12 Books To Furnish

CW01467108

12 Books To Furnish A Room

Simon Barnes

© Simon Barnes 2024

The individual pieces by originally appeared in *The Newsletter* and *Secret Harmonies,* published by The Anthony Powell Society.

The introduction is © The Anthony Powell Society

The cover, which was designed by Two Associates, based on photographs by and © Cindy Lee Wright, is © The Anthony Powell Society.

Simon Barnes has asserted his right to be identified as the author of this work in accordance with the Copyright, Designs and Patents Act, 1988.

Published by The Anthony Powell Society
Four Hatches
Friday Street
Lower Quinton
Stratford Upon Avon CV37 8SQ

ISBN 978-0-9956267-9-9

Printed and bound in Wellingborough, UK, by Lonsdale Direct Solutions.

Dedication

It's for Rooby (you fool!)

A novelist writes what he is. That is equally true of authors who deal with mediaeval romance or journeys to the moon.

X Trapnel

Introduction: In Praise of Journalists

Anthony Powell valued writing fiction. Of course he did. As a novelist he wrote, as X Trapnel pronounced and Simon Barnes reminds us, what he was. But it was his journalism that kept his head above water. The regular cheques from The Telegraph made the difference between washing down his luncheon with grocer's claret from Frome and with something special from Mayfair, delivered through the silent country lanes in a discreet van.

I once informed Richard Barry, the editor of a magazine for which I occasionally wrote, that I had read many novels and the best by and large were those written by writers who were also journalists. Of course, he said, you're right; you have to drag the reader in with your first para – just because they've paid doesn't mean they're going to read you - and if you aren't writing against a deadline, silliness creeps in.

Richard never made anything up in his life. It was one of his strengths as an investigative journalist. He didn't really know what he was talking about when he came to fiction. He was right though.

I love Powell's journalism. For the Society I have edited two volumes – they are published as *Anthony Powell On Wine* and *King Arthur And Other Personages* - and we are working on a third. So I have read quite a lot of it. They are mainly book reviews. He accepts the writers on whom he comments at their own estimation. Sometimes he corrects them tetchily, if, for instance, they confuse the form of address for the daughter of a peer with that that for the wife of a knight, but he doesn't tell them what, as regards the thrust of their work, they meant to say or should have said. He is hilariously scrupulous, even with *The Holy Blood and the Holy Grail*, the work that inspired Dan Brown. See *King Arthur*. He would seize on absurdities and he would fashion digressions. He would amuse. He was in his quiet way joyful. And it was all done, as you would expect, with aristocratic disinterest – or at least what appeared to be aristocratic disinterest.

Was he, you might ask, in his pieces for The Telegraph, Bernard Shernmaker or Nathaniel Sheldon, the two literary commentators in *Books Do Furnish A Room*? Shernmaker (a great name, by the way) was self-consciously a Critic. He knew better than the writers on whom he opined. He was up to what they were up to. Sheldon on the other hand was a jobbing commentator. Sheldon would have turned in a thousand words on *Whither Meghan Markle?*, as would my editor Richard – Shernmaker, never. And Powell? He was like neither, I think. He loved the work and the craft, as Sheldon didn't, and he loved it too much, unlike Shernmaker, to bully. He was sufficiently confident in his own stature as a writer, not to mention his contractual arrangements with The Telegraph, to stoop to tittle-tattle.

Simon Barnes has a significant background writing for The Times and other publications, as well as his books. Would he agree, if paid enough, to turn in a thousand words on *Whither Meghan Markle?* I dare say that he might. Evelyn Waugh certainly did that sort of thing, and his incidental and often very trivial journalism has been collected by Oxford University Press, long *post mortem*, into a single volume, which will cost you £135. Shernmaker would have accepted an offer to edit that collection, to explain what Waugh should have said and how it all fitted into the *zeitgeist*.

I am always amazed, incidentally, when I reread *Books*, how Powell imagined an entire alternative literary universe for late 1940s London: the critics, the writers, the politics, even the magazines. Most writers (Waugh, for example) would have fallen back on real people or real people thinly disguised. Powell instead gives us a whole imagined world, scrupulously imagined so that it makes sense to one who knows the era, but imagined nonetheless, just as he had done with the music world in *Casanova's Chinese Restaurant*. There is no Tambimuttu, thank goodness. Simon passionately asserts, in the first piece below, the novelist's duty to make things up, as Powell so consummately does, and the reader's concomitant duty to take the writer at his word.

It seems to me too that, presented with such a glorious alternative universe, to spend one's time debating whether it requires to be footnoted with supposed 'character models' is, to say the least of it, rude.

Sheldon, taking his cue from our sternly moralistic opinion-formers, would, if he were alive today, treat the characters in such novels as he noticed as prospective role models, and mark them appropriately: diversity 6/10, soundness as to Gaza 3/10, and so on. Shernmaker might have disappeared into such rabbit holes as semiotics and be lost to sight, but let us assume not. I think that he would be explaining how he would have written *Dance* (say) differently and how much better. He would describe the *zeitgeist* of the period during which the novel was written – the particular moral, political and philosophical obsessions. He would add the writer to a list of other writers with, as he identified them, similar aims, whom either he blessed or was regrettably required to correct.

As Powell complains from time to time in the *Journals,* that - like it or not - is not how novelists work; critics often seem simply not to understand how novelists work.

To which I would add that, since critics are paid to read books, in a way that no one else is, they are often immune to clunky first paragraphs, they don't recognise silliness creeping in and they are, in short, dead to good writing. You can tell from the way that they tend to write themselves. For example, critics routinely inform us that Waugh 'never wrote a dull sentence'. One's reaction as often as not is: 'How on earth can you tell?'

Here we have a selection of pieces written by Simon Barnes about Powell's work and specifically about *Dance*. He is at pains to say that he is not a critic. Shernmaker's condescension is foreign to him.

He revels in the work, sometimes he wallows in it; he might have written it himself given such things as time, opportunity and genius. He comes at the novel at ninety degrees and illuminates it as no one else could – although different ninety-degree approaches are available to us all. Shernmaker would never have thought of Widmerpool as a greyhound. And Widmerpool-as-a-greyhound illuminates things - that is the point - in a way that Shernmaker's *zeitgeist* never will. See *An Evening At Wimbledon Dogs*.

Simon honours his journalistic background, and, indirectly, Powell's too. His opening paras (as are Powell's) are impeccable. Word count never falters. Imagination flourishes but silliness is under firm control.

Powell, alas, never lived to see Widmerpool's self-satisfied features grafted in imagination onto the fit body of a racing dog. That is a privilege reserved for the readers of this book. But he did, as recorded above, read that Jesus and Mary Magdelene founded the Merovingian royal family, a bloodline that is still secretly and excitingly with us. His reaction would I think have been the same now as then:

I am a pushover for this sort of fantasy.

Robin Bynoe

5

Foreword

No, I am not Bernard Shernmaker, nor was meant to be. Shernmaker turns up to the launch of *Fission* in the tenth volume of *A Dance to the Music of Time*: "Indeed one of his goals was to establish finally that the Critic, not the Author, was paramount."

I am no critic. I'm a reader. There are only two people who matter when it comes to novels: the writer and the reader. But readers aren't always alone. We can have conversations, united by our relationship with the book. And that's what I have been doing with the pieces that follow: having a conversation with fellow-members of the Anthony Powell Society, one made possible by the *Newsletter* and *Secret Harmonies*.

Were they trying to make a critic of me when I was reading English at university? The theme of loss in *Hamlet*. *The Waste Land* is a poem about hope: discuss. What is the role of courtly love in *Sir Gawain and the Green Knight?* They gave me a third and lucky to get that. Failing to make the grade as a critic, I had no option. I was forced to become a writer.

Sometimes people ask for advice: how can I become a writer myself? My answer is always the same.

Read. Never stop reading. Read your favourite authors, read your specialist subject, read subjects that catch your fancy, read authors your friends recommend, go back to old favourites, read *The Divine Comedy, Finnegans Wake*, James Bond, football match reports, Darwin, Narnia, *The Cricketer, War and Peace*, Harry Potter, and if you've got nothing better you can even read *How to Be a Bad Birdwatcher* by Simon Barnes.

It was my brother-in-law Rob (Rooby in the family) who told me I should read the *Dance*; that was about 1980. After a suitable interval I gave it a go and quite liked it. In a few months I had read the first three volumes and was starting number four. And then, in the first chapter of that volume, I ran headlong into a Powellian coincidence that seemed to rip the universe from end to end. Suddenly I understood what fiction on this massive scale is all about. I read the rest of the *Dance* in a few weeks and then started at the beginning again – and I've been doing that ever since, though I've read quite a lot of other stuff as well.

The next time I bumped into Rooby was at a curious hotel in Bangkok (its curious nature unknown to us when we booked). I saw him across the swimming-pool and greeted him: "The essence of the all is the godhead of the true." Most readers will have little difficulty in guessing his reply.

Every first reading is a reconnaissance. If the book is any good you can come back to it again and again: reminding yourself of marvellous things while forever finding new ones. I look forward to the next time I start again with the workmen round their brazier and Widmerpool running out of the mist. In the meantime, let me continue this conversation with a few thoughts about *A Dance to the Music of Time*.

Simon Barnes

Contents

The Heresy Of Fiction

I had a sudden urge to turn into X Trapnel. I wanted to be in the pub, pissed and verbose, haranguing Nick Jenkins and Books Bagshaw about novels and how we write them. I wanted to shout down Bagshaw and go spiralling off from Nick's more thoughtful points; I wanted to lay down the law about fiction and the way that writers of fiction put their books together.

This intemperate response was triggered by a review of two more books about Evelyn Waugh, one by Ann Pasternak Slater and one by Philip Eade. (Does Nick's/Powell's theory of self-pity as the most popular quality in fiction explain Waugh's traditionally higher place in the 20th century hit parade?)

The Pasternak book got a bit of rave. The reviewer made much of the correlations between Waugh's life and Waugh's fiction, the way that Waugh's own experiences are reflected in his fiction, and the extent to which his characters – even the most extravagant apparent caricatures – are based on people he actually met.

And all this is intriguing. In this magazine we often read equally intriguing pieces about Powell's life, his friends and his acquaintances, and speculate privately or openly about their relationship with the *Dance* and other fiction.

So sure, it's *interesting* to consider the similarities and the differences between Constant Lambert and Hugh Moreland, and the extent to which Reginald Manningham Butler or Edward Heath were inspirations for Widmerpool... just is it's interesting to consider how closely Nora Barnacle resembles Molly Bloom in *Ulysses*, and how much influence James Joyce's schizophrenic daughter Lucia had on *Finnegans Wake*.

But then the chest-prodding ranting inner Trapnel broke free, and I wanted to shout to the uninterested saloon bar: "For Christ's sake, aren't we allowed to make anything up?"

Trapnel spoke about the Heresy of Naturalism: "People can't get it right about Naturalism. They think a writer like me writes the sort of books I do because it's easier, or necessary nowadays. You just look around at what's happening and shove it all down. They can't understand that it's not in the least the case. It's just as selective, just as artificial, as if the characters were kings and queens speaking in blank verse."

So let me thump my pint down on the table and expound on the Heresy of Fiction. The heresy is the belief that authors like Waugh, like Powell, like Trapnel and for that matter like me, don't actually make anything up at all. It's all transmuted from experience. We just shove it all down. All characters have their real-life counter-parts. Sometimes they can even be used twice, like Captain Bromwich (*What's*

Become of Waring) and Dicky Umfraville, or Books himself and Fotheringham (*Afternoon Men*). At the very most we allow an author credit for combining two or three people of his acquaintance into a single composite. Everything in fiction has an explanation from life. Every roman has its clef.

I have had four novels published. No one is going to write my biography and trace my characters from the people I have known in my life, or trace the incidents of my life that have been turned into incidents in these novels. There will never be a Simon Barnes Society. But that hasn't made me immune to the Heresy of Fiction. I still get no credit for making things up.

My favourite comment on my first-born, *Rogue Lion Safaris*, was: "I didn't know you could drive." I was enraptured by this. Because I can't drive, neither could Dan Lynch, the narrator of *Rogue Lion*. He can drive; his author can't. Glad it all seemed so convincing, but I've never put a Land Cruiser into low-ratio in my life.

My least favourite comment was really rather troubling: "I always knew you'd fucked her." Certainly, Dan and Caro have a fling in the course of the novel: the author didn't. Caro's appearance came from a picture of a *jolie-laide* (though not one with *beauté de singe*) in a chance-found copy of *Vogue*, the rest of her came from sources that elude me; I have forgotten them if I ever knew. I made her up, you see. And for the rest, should it really come as news to anyone that it's possible for a human being to *imagine* having sex?

An unsympathetic review of my third novel, *Miss Chance*, complained about the passages in which the lead male character is seen as a performance poet, saying that they obviously came from personal experience, which was an added reason to despise them. The biographical truth is that I have never read a poem of mine to an audience in my life. I made it up. I imagined it. I invented something and then I wrote it down. That's how you write novels. I needed the character to have a love of performance, and I needed him to be in a small way a star, so that he could be eclipsed by the far greater talents of the woman he marries. So I made him stand up in front of an audience and recite *The Night of Serial Buttock-Fondling* to an undergraduate audience during the interval at a concert. I never did that myself, thank God. Not that stupid. Or brave.

Yes, sure, I've taken people from real life and put them into novels. George Sorensen, the safari guide in *Rogue Lion Safaris*, is based on my dear and late friend Bob -- Baron Robert Stjernstedt -- but I toned him down to make him believable. I also made him an ethologist – a student of animal behaviour – rather than an ornithologist. I then made him the author of the definitive work on lion behaviour, *Lions of the Plains*. The book actually exists, but it was written by the real -- and great -- ethologist George Schaller; and is called *The Serengeti Lion: A Study of Predator-Prey Relations*. But George Sorensen isn't George Schaller any more than he's Bob Stjernstedt.

13

The combination was a starting point: after that I made stuff up.

Miss Chance is a what-if novel: what if she hadn't given me the elbow? What if she'd married me instead? But again, that was just the starting-point. I didn't just dredge up memories of the lady in question and shove them all down. I changed her. I made her a successful writer, a fair bit nastier, an awful lot madder and a very great deal more promiscuous.

Before your experience can become a novel, the characters go through a process that's hard to explain and one that non-writers seem reluctant to understand. Sure, they started out as Bob and as Mlle X, but by the time they hit the page, they are George and Morgan. You're not transcribing life line by line and letter by letter, as Trapnel himself points out when he talks about finding a tape-recording of a tender scene between lovers.

No. You're making it up. And the best part of the process comes when you stop having to work at it. You stop putting words into their mouths and actions into their lives and start, as it were, to take dictation. Not from life but from places that lie deeper than conscious thought.

Let's not get mystical about it. Trapnel would hate that. No sacred mysteries: Trapnel was (or is) tremendously keen to see writing as a job of work, a craft to be discussed and honed and improved. But there comes a point in writing fiction when the characters take on an illusory life in the author's mind. There's a character in Trapnel's destroyed masterpiece *Profiles In String* based on Pamela Widmerpool, but it wasn't a historical record of her life. Perhaps that's why Pam thought the book unworthy of X. Perhaps her problem was that she was too literal-minded. That's one explanation.

The characters and actions of a novel aren't entirely under the author's conscious control. That's another thing that non-writers never seem to grasp. Your characters have, or seem to have, a will and/or a destiny of their own. I remember telling an author of detective fiction that I envied and admired the skills of plotting and preplanning that such a writer must have. Not a bit of it, she told me. She was in deep difficulties with her current book because she had just realised that the villain couldn't possibly have done it.

That's how fiction works. People you meet, experiences you have, incidents you observe: these come into fiction all right, but they tend to be starting points. Once you start writing them you don't appropriate them, you change them. They become fiction. They become fiction because the author makes them up.

The fascination for an author's raw material is like studying an athlete's training regimen. Training is important, highly significant, and you can't perform without it, but in the end it doesn't matter. It's not what a batsman does in the nets that counts: it's what happens in the match, out in the middle, facing the bowling. In sport we are aware of this important difference: but not, it seems in literature. What matters in a novel is not where the material came from but what the novelist does with it. And that's the process of making things up. It's what novelists do. It's what no one accepts that novelists do.

Never mind. I have, many times in my life, been praised for making things up. One example will suffice. Years ago, I interviewed a surfer, who told me: "The wave has come to you across thousands miles of ocean and no one will ride it except you. Surf it, and it's gone. You have a relationship with a wave, a complete involvement with it, and then it's broken. You know those insects that mate once and then die? It's like that."

So inevitably somebody asked me: "Great line. Brilliant. I don't suppose he really said that, did he?"

Always, when I'm writing non-fiction, in newspapers and magazines and books, I stick to the plonking pedantic literal truth. The principle is not moral, or at least, not moral in a mustn't-tell-lies way. There is a permanent temptation to twist every tale to fit the banal formats of newspaper stories: heroic policeman, dirty vicar, innocent victim, evil foreigner, cute animal. The truth tends to be more interesting and more complex: and more difficult to write.

But you never get the credit for that. Write the truth -- shove it all down -- and people believe that you're a writer of fiction. Write fiction and everybody believes it's a literal, plonking, pedantic record of

16

what happened. And that is the Heresy of Fiction. Now buy me another pint and then help me home.

Because I can't drive.

What Maisky Knew
Non-Human Animals In *Dance*

So what about the animals in *A Dance to the Music of Time*? Not the most obvious question, I know, but it's one that intrigues me. I have written many books about wildlife, and have just completed *The History of the World in 100 Animals*. I have written two and half books about horses (the half being *The Horse: A Celebration in Art*, a collaboration with my sister Rachel, who knows about art). Lions, birds and horses play important roles in three of my novels. I have ridden and owned horses most of my life.

So naturally I find myself looking for the beasts at the *Dance*: the non-human animals who make fleeting appearances in the pages, revealing aspects of their own lives and shedding light on the doings of the human dancers who trot and prance, take wing and come down to earth across the 12-volume ballroom... also revealing certain things about the author and his manner of working.

Powell was famously devoted to cats, but only two characters in Dance are allowed cats, and only one cat has a name. That apart, animals didn't play much part in Powell's life, although Hilary Spurling reports that in his later youth he rode regularly when staying with his parents, more to combat boredom than enthusiasm for the horsey life. On one occasion the horse took off with him, giving him a fright and the idea for Arthur Zouch's accident in *From a View to a Death*.

So let's turn to the *Dance* and take it one volume at a time, patting the non-human characters as we go.

A Question of Upbringing

The most important non-humans in the first volume are Charley and Bum, the dogs who live chez Leroy. What is striking is the way that the narrator treats the relationship between the two dogs with the same detached seriousness he employs for human relationships. "Charley was never washed, and resenting this attention to his fellow, would on this account pick a quarrel with Bum every seven days."

In his brief observations on the dogs Jenkins is revealed as a sort of naturalist, a dispassionate observer of life around him. He can be compared to David Attenborough in the great *Life* trilogy, especially *The Trials of Life*, his classic series on ethology, the science of animal behaviour. Attenborough's role of observer and teller of the stories is varied with passages of participation and even occasional moments of passionate involvement. Jenkins, more or less by definition uninvolved, finds himself in dismaying scenes of passion with Jean in *The Acceptance World*; in the same way that

Attenborough famously enjoyed his encounter with gorillas in *Life on Earth*.

Bum plays a more active role a little later when he escapes from his bath and is pursued by Suzette and Jenkins, a chase that ends in a lightning-brief moment of hand-holding intimacy, before Widmerpool intervenes.

Another animal plays an off-stage but decisive role in the story. This is the horse that Stringham rides when he is in Kenya. He draws the horse for Nick in a letter: anticipating the time when Stringham is being cured of drink by means of therapeutic painting in gouache. Alas, the horse – it's presumably the same one -- "throws" -- an old euphemism for falling off – Stringham a few days before he is to return to England. He is laid up for some months, and doesn't arrive in Oxford until the summer term, whereupon he takes "against the place at once". The horse ensures that he is out of step with the world: and he chooses (doesn't he?) to remain that way.

A Buyer's Market

Sultan is the presiding animal of this volume: Eleanor Walpole-Wilson's Labrador. It is (presumably) Sultan's need for exercise that takes Eleanor and Barbara into Kensington Garden with the dog, and so makes possible the – as it were – Arcadian idyll, in which Nick comes across girls and dog by chance. "Oh, what fun to meet like this," says

Barbara, precipitating Nick into the anguish of unrequited love.

Sultan is present a few pages later at the dinner given by Eleanor's parents, when Archie Gilbert helps Eleanor to propel him into his wicker hutch, heedless of the beauty of his own evening clothes. Archie's perfection of turnout is clearly not a matter of narcissism but an aspect of his boundless willingness to oblige.

Later in the book Eleanor tries to get out of the Stourwater excursion because she wants to see some hound puppies. At Stourwater, Johnny Pardoe borrows her dog-chain to restrain Rosie Manasch in the dungeons, a jape that pleases some of the company more than others. Eleanor "appeared to be enjoying herself for the first time since our arrival at the castle."

The Acceptance World

No animal appears directly on stage in the third volume, but the horsey world – perhaps in its way a branch of the Acceptance World, for certainly when you own a horse you're never quite sure on what terms business will be transacted – is crucial to the last part of this volume, for it's horses that bring Foppa and Dicky Umfraville together, propelling Umfraville into the narrative of *Dance*.

Umfraville had encountered Foppa at the trotting races; and there is a photograph in Foppa's club of Foppa taking part in one of these races, "his small person almost hidden between the tail of his horse and the giant wheels of the sulky". Sulky, the correct term for such a two-wheeled cart, is produced with surprising nonchalance, the only sign that Jenkins knows anything at all about horses. This alliance between these two horsey men causes a division between Barnby and Anne Stepney while seeming to push Nick and Jean Templar towards their passionate finale.

There is a faint touch of animal life at the Isbister retrospective exhibition. Bijou Ardglass is seen admiring her own equestrian portrait, her horse bearing the charmingly ironical name of Faithful Girl. (Was it reckless of Isbister to paint a horse? Horses are notoriously difficult subjects and are usually left to specialists. Perhaps that recklessness was at the heart of Isbister's failure to be anything more than a "society painter".) We also learn that Eleanor Walpole-Wilson is now living in the country where "her breeding keeps her quiet". Sultan has died and Eleanor is breeding Labradors.

At Lady Molly's

The book opens with a discussion of General Conyers and the archaic kind of horsiness that still surrounds him: victory in the Military Cup and most notably, his part in the Boer War when "the whole Cavalry Division was ordered to charge". The General himself talks about the charge in the closing pages of the book, revealing his less than glamorous part: "I had the greatest difficulty in getting my pony out of a trot".

22

The General trains poodles as gundogs. This fact is offered as an example of his eccentricity, his determination to carry through unusual projects. But there is also a faintly subversive note here: by preferring poodles to traditional gundogs he is suggesting that intelligence and education are more significant than ancestry. This is not a view reflected in the General's social life, or, apparently, his political life.

Maisky, Molly's monkey, first appears in this volume. As with Charley and Bum, Jenkins views him with the same ironical detachment as the human characters: "There was something of Quiggin in his seriousness and self-absorption."

Miss Weedon then remarks that she doesn't care for monkeys. Both she and Molly are great looker-afterers, but in this declaration of "anti-simianism" Tuffy makes it clear that her notion of caring is rather different from Molly's. Molly cares recklessly for anybody who crosses her path: Miss Weedon is highly selective and focused. She has already explained how she is helping Stringham to be cured of drink; in later volumes she takes on (in marriage) General Conyers and Sonny Farebrother. In her, power and love seem inextricable.

Miss Weedon tells Nick that Lord Amesbury turned up at Molly's in knee-breeches and the Garter, and shared scrambled eggs with Molly's vet, who has come to treat a cat with fever; you never know who you might meet at Lady Molly's. When the General and Nick have their conversation about Widmerpool's adventures in love, they do so in Molly's boudoir, surrounded by cats sitting "in an ill-humoured group".

Casanova's Chinese Restaurant

This novel is so intensely London that it never leaves Zone 1. You could walk round every location in the book in half a day, tracing the stroll made by Nick and Moreland after supper with the Maclinticks in Pimlico. As a result, non-human life scarcely gets a mention. St John Clarke, in the course of lunch with Lady Warminster, says that he finds listening to the "confabulations of sparrows" more amusing than writing his memoirs – before remembering that he is a Man of the Left, correcting himself with more robust sentiments. At the same lunch, Lady Warminster remarks that Stringham's father, Boffles, looked "wonderful on a horse".

Later, at the party given for Moreland's symphony, Stringham encounters Mrs Maclintick, addresses her as "Bo-Peep" and asks what has happened to her sheep.

The Kindly Ones

The first chapter is set in the country, at Stonehurst near Aldershot, and a few animals managed to creep in. One is the horse ridden by the military policeman. Nick's father is introduced to us in the middle of one of his disasters as he is about to set off hunting. We learn that he, like Stringham, is "thrown", but without taking much harm and

24

retaining his eyeglass. This leads to a classic Powellian reflection that in depicting his father as "a fox-hunter wearing an eyeglass" he risks giving a false impression: "indeed a totally erroneous one". The unreliable nature of fact is made clear.

In the following chapter, Nick and his wife pay a visit to Moreland and Matty, who are now living in the country without much apparent relish for such a life. Moreland, low in spirits, spends much of his time "nursing a large tabby cat called Farinelli". This is the only cat in the Dance with a name – and it's a perfect name for Moreland's cat: Farinelli was the great castrato singer of the 18th century. As the party advances on Stourwater they observe the black swans in the moat: a species native to Australia, as Moreland points out. I have seen them on the Torrens River, when covering Test matches in Adelaide.

Moreland turns up unexpectedly in the last chapter: Molly meets him at the vets when both are trying to "rehome" – is that a euphemism for euthanising? -- various pets. So as the war begins, and Moreland is deprived of his wife, his home and even his chief comforter. Farinelli's passing from the narrative does, with the lightest of Powellian touches, tell about the cruelties of both love and of war.

The Valley of Bones

Total war brings us very few animals. General Liddament's dogs appear offstage, an aspect of his calculated informality. Here is a hint for any readers who wish to pass themselves off as upper-class: you should always be accompanied by two Jack Russells, dogs permanently beyond all human control and for whom no apology is ever made. Jenkins's platoon overnights while on exercise in what might have been a cow barn. "What nasty smells there are here," Corporal Gwylt complains. "I do not like all these cows." Bithel's attic smells of mice.

When Jenkins visits Frederica's house on weekend leave from his course, he remeets Dicky Umfraville, and it's here we have that lovely line, never forgotten by any horsey people who read Powell: Umfraville's face "possessed that look of innate sadness which often marks the features of those habituated the boundless unreliability of horses." I quoted that phrase in my second book, which was based round a year in the life of a racing stable, in reference to the trainer John Dunlop.

The Soldier's Art

General Liddament's dogs make a more telling appearance in this volume. Widmerpool refers to them (and the hunting horns the general carries) as "pure affectation". But we learn that Widmerpool was "not above saying wuff-wuff to the pair of them", and to giving them "unconvincing pats of encouragement". In this passage we learn that Widmerpool "dislikes all animals". This small, almost thrown away observation skewers Widmerpool for all time. Our pet animals are a perpetual opportunity for the giving and receiving of affection. Are there are any characters, human or non-human, for whom Widmerpool feels genuine affection? He is variously smitten with Barbara, Gypsy and Pamela, but being smitten isn't the same thing as affection.

Certainly he speaks affectionately of his mother, in the early volumes at least; which makes his later treatment of her particularly telling. At other times, his interest in other people is directly related to their usefulness.

Perhaps the only exception is Nick himself. Widmerpool does seem to have an ungainly liking for Nick, taking the trouble to invite him for lunch with very little ulterior motive. Nick's determination -- insofar as such a word can be used of him – to live in a different manner and by different values to Widmerpool exerts on Widmerpool some kind of fascination, and is perhaps that is at the heart of the curious bond between them.

This, as it were, unconsummated affection is perhaps what prompts Widmerpool to select Nick as his assistant in this volume. It is a period of unprecedented intimacy that dispels any last trace of affection between them.

The Military Philosophers

When Nick accompanies a group of military attaches to France "pour les vacances", there is brief glimpse of a "small cart pulled by a muscular-looking dog." Here is a brief vignette of foreignness: of exoticism after the long years of being cooped-up by the still uncompleted war. It's a mildly comical companion-piece to the vignette of the bearded

Frenchman that reduces Nick – briefly, as he is keen to point out – to tears. The cart-pulling dog stands for the fun, the unexpected nature, the total unEnglishness of abroad: a thing much missed. War had perhaps stressed, to an uncomfortable degree, the insularity of the English.

This volume also reports the death of Maisky, the monkey. He was - apparently – euthanised after biting the hand of Smith the butler as both attempted to claim the same nut. Smith died of consequent septicaemia. There is a perfectly unstated comic element to this: it's not the way you might except to die during a war. Nick had mused earlier in the sequence about the sometimes appropriate nature of a person's death: here perhaps is another example.

After hearing this story, narrated by Ted Jeavons, Nick glances at a snapshot of Molly "wearing a Fair Isle jumper and holding Maisky like a baby". Here is Molly, the tireless and childless mother to all the world, caught for all time. "Maisky, heedless of mortality, looked infinitely self-satisfied."

There is a slightly odd passage in this volume, during the great air-raid, when Jenkins encounters Pamela in the hallway of his block of flats. "Pamela Flitton gave the impression of being thoroughly vicious, using the world not so much in the moral sense, but as one might speak of a horse – specifically a mare." Vicious by nature rather than by choice. It's an old horsey saying that you can't school (i.e. teach) temperament, but the idea that any horse is innately vicious doesn't ring true to a horseman. I'm not sure I have ever encountered a horse that was vicious by nature. I have met horses that could be overwhelming, or spiteful, or genuinely dangerous, but there is always a back-story (known or unknown) to explain this. If that's so with Pamela, we never hear that story. We know that her father Cosmo Flitton was a swine (Dicky Umfraville is to be trusted in this diagnosis) and we learn later that her mother suffered a series of nervous illness. She was a difficult child and was sick in the font at her uncle Charles Stringham's wedding. But what was her story? What made her "vicious"?

Books Do Furnish a Room

X.Trapnel called his novel *Camel Ride to the Tomb*. This was the repeated cry of cry of a man recommending his own form of "archaeological transport". Trapnel explains: "I grasped at once that was what life was. How could the description be bettered? Juddering through the wilderness, on an uncomfortable conveyance you can't properly control, along a rocky, unpremeditated, but indefeasible track, toward the destination crudely, yet truly, stated."

I once rode a camel trained to perform dressage moves and was much taken by the animal's willingness and charm. Trapnel's title is a great metaphor, but unfair to camels.

We also learn that Trapnel's father worked as a jockey in the Near East. The pay-off line to the entire volume – a sentence that even on its own is a good enough reason for reading and recommending the entire series – is a masterpiece. Dicky Umfraville has inevitably heard of the racing exploits of Trapnel père: "I once won a packet on a horse of his called Amour Piquant."

Temporary Kings

Non-human life plays no part in this volume, neither in Venice nor London. Not so much as a pigeon, save in the cover illustration of the hardback. Never mind: Powell makes up for it in the one that follows.

Hearing Secret Harmonies

The television adaptation of *Dance* was widely criticised because in the final of the four episodes, covering the last three volumes, Nick was played by a different actor, destroying all sense of continuity. But there is precedent: the Nick of the final volume has, like Bottom, been translated. Our lurking, brooding, observing ethologist-urbanite has suddenly turned into a country gent. And as a result of these country matters, the first chapter is a great detonation on non-human life.

The very first word of the book is "duck". They land as a flock, and settle on the water, reminding Nick of a discussion about ducks between two generals in *The Military Philosophers*. Later, when walking home from the crayfishing expedition with Scorp Murtlock, the ducks rise together, again in formation, and both men wonder what the birds foretell. I am mildly troubled by this. These events take place in mid-to-late June or early July: at least that's the assumption, for Murtlock says that it is "too near the solstice" to leap the fire. A fortnight either side of June 21 seems fair. Ducks don't go in for much flocking behaviour at this time; it's the heart of the breeding season and most of them are therefore in pairs, not all together in a flock. What Nick sees is far from impossible, but the flocking that excited the generals presumably took place during the shooting season – winter, when ducks love to be in large numbers. It all depends on what Nick/Powell means by flock. Half a dozen, fine: 50-odd, unlikely.

Nick also mentions twice that he can smell fox: quite a trick that. In my experience women are better at picking up the whiff than men. Nick is piling on his country street-cred -- well, green-lane-cred -- pretty thick.

The crayfish are described with great accuracy, presumably from experience: "swart miniature lobsters... macabre knowing demeanour". They are, I think, the British species of white-clawed crayfish; the fact that these are historic crayfish beds is confirmed by Mr Gauntlet, who used to catch them. It was round about this time or a little later – early 70s – that British farmers were encouraged to diversify into the raising of signal crayfish from America; they got out and now out-compete the British species.

I worry about those poor horses. Nick reports that the caravan that carries Murtlock and the rest is pulled "by a pair of sound greys". The classic gypsy caravan is drawn by a single horse, but perhaps this was a larger vehicle.

31

But how did they manage the journey? Nick estimates that they travel 20 miles a day, a fair old distance, day after day. Do the party have an obliging relative with free grazing every 20 miles? Or at worst, accommodation with some – presumably last year's – hay? And surely they will need short feed -- with more protein -- as well: these horses are seriously working for their living, and need fuel. They can't do it all by grazing the roadsides. Who did the organising? Who is horseman enough to manage this sound pair? Who checks their feet? How did they find a farrier when necessary? Horse management is not an easy job at all, and I can't see any of the four in that role. At the end of the chapter, Murtlock mentions that "Barnabas must water the horses". I hope very much that the horses had been watered already: if they had already covered 20 miles that day, a drink would be the first requirement when work is over, not an afterthought. But perhaps Barnabas was merely topping up the drinking-place he had already established.

A kestrel appears, and Nick one-ups Murtlock by claiming to recognise the kestrel as an individual, boldly stating that the bird is male. Kestrels are sexually dimorphic, so maybe Nick picked that up – for all we know, he might be carrying top-of-the-range binoculars. "That particular one is always hanging about," he says. It is likely that at this time of the year, male and female will be both involved in raising chicks and feeding young; both adults will be very active and often seen. But let's say Nick is a good enough birder to sex kestrels at long range.

We also hear that Eleanor Walpole-Wilson has died and left Norah a pair of noisy dogs: "Shut-up pugs." It's nice vignette of the Norah's combative disposition.

We then move on, in this Noah's ark of a chapter, to find Mr Gauntlett looking for his Labrador, Daisy. He seems to be a bit careless with dogs: every time Daisy is about to pup she manages to get out and litter in the woods. Murtlock tells him to appease the shades of his dwelling. He should also have told him to close the door of his dwelling and keep a better eye on his dog.

Murtlock spookily knows just where Daisy is lying up, as it later turns out. The words of the seer come to him in what looks to Nick like a brief trance, and we see that Murtlock's supernatural credentials are at least in part genuine. The way he makes so little of this adds a curious touch: he finds his own powers in this instance no big deal. The chapter ends with Nick and Isobel agreeing on Murtlock's creepy nature.

We are back in the country in chapter 5. Mr Gauntlett remarks on the correctness of Murtlock's prediction of Daisy's whereabouts: Mr Gauntlett found her with one pup still alive. Was this the result of a casual union with a village mutt? If this was a planned mating with another gundog, Mr Gauntlett would presumably have been more careful.

He explains that Ernie Dunch had seen Murtlock's group at their midsummer rites. Dunch had been shooting rabbits from his Land-Rover in the dark, though we later learn that Murtlock's group were unaware of this.

When Ernie gets back, traumatised, we hear that he started every time one of the "young owls hooted". Why *young* owls? At Midsummer, you are far more likely to hear the sound of mature owls, hooting to safeguard their breeding territory. These are presumably tawny owls, far more active in late night than other species; barn own are mostly crepuscular (dawn and dusk), and besides, they don't hoot. The time for hearing young owls – recognisable from their rather amateurish attempts at hooting – is autumn, when birds have left the parental territory and are looking for a vacant place where they can settle. Perhaps Powell is overdoing the green-lane-cred with this detail. Or perhaps Mr Gauntlett is: overacting his own part of "professional rusticity".

Nick and Gwinnett, encountered by chance, later look down from the summit of the hill to Murtlock's caravan. If the horses are in sight, they are not mentioned. Again, I hope Barnabas -- or someone – has been doing a proper job with them. Even if you have spent all night trying to raise the dead, the horses still need food and water.

I set about these observations because non-human life is a major preoccupation of mine, and so is the *Dance*. Non-human life played very little part in Powel's life and works, so perhaps the idea of tracing the animals in Dance is a little silly. But by looking at things from an unexpected point of view – as you do when you come on someone you know unexpectedly – you can catch them unawares. By looking at the Powellian menagerie, I feel as if I have caught the novel off its guard.

And there are small points that reveal just how good a novelist Powell is. In a few acute phrases, Charley, Bum and Maisky live: and by doing so reveal more of the human characters around them.

The science of ethology was just getting into its stride as Powell was writing the final novel of *Dance* (*Hearing Secret Harmonies* was published in 1975: Jane Goodall began working with chimpanzees in 1960, Dian Fossey with gorillas in 1966, George Schaller with lions in 1966, Cynthia Moss with elephants in 1968.)

The method of the ethologist is to get your studied animals accustomed to an observing presence. You must be completely accepted, and yet wholly uninvolved. You are there to record, not to participate. Perhaps this approach sounds familiar to readers of the *Dance*.

Ethology begins with the observer's ability to recognise each member of the studied group as an individual. That leads to the perennial dilemma is how to refer to them. Some researchers give them names, an approach that might compromise objectivity and encourage the deadly sin of anthropomorphism. Others prefer numbers, which might damage empathy.

But in a sense that's what Powell does. He doesn't actually refer to Moreland as Seven or Jean as Three, but he always insists on a certain formality when it comes to names. Moreland is never referred to as Hugh outside inverted commas, Matilda is never Matty, Sillery never Sillers, Bithel never Bith and Bagshaw never Books, though presumably Nick uses all these forms of address. Widmerpool invites Nick to call him Kenneth, but remains Widmerpool in the text.

In his observations of human and non-human life, Powell remains the ethologist: forever seeking an objectivity that is ultimately unattainable. You must understand the nature of the attempt, and its inevitable failure, if you wish to grasp the secret of the *Dance*. Like every good work of ethology, it is a work of the most passionate detachment.

The Social Climber As Hero

We're accustomed to think of the social climber in fiction as a fairly grotesque character: broadly comic, a bit pathetic, fundamentally unsympathetic... and that's why we completely miss the social climber when we run across him as hero. Perhaps that's because the reader identifies with such heroes. Perhaps that's because the author does as well.

So let's look at three major past-war works of fiction: the *Dance, Brideshead Revisited* and *Lucky Jim*. Each of these works contains a social climber who can be despised, mocked and laughed at: a character who enhances the reader's self-esteem (and that, Powellian readers should note, is at least as helpful a trick in popular fiction as self-pity).

Each of these three characters is, in a different way, a work of genius. These despicable social climbers are Widmerpool (of course), Rex Mottram and Bertrand Welch. We'll look at them in a moment: and after we've done so I'll suggest that all three members of this glorious trio conceal the fact that the heroes of these three works are also all social climbers to a man. The ultimately failed social-climbing of the first three sets off the gloriously successful social climbing of the heroes: that is to say, Nick Jenkins, Charles Ryder and Jim Dixon.

But before we move on, I'd like to make it pedantically clear that these observations are not intended as destructive criticisms of three great works. I am not attempting any sort of attack on any of them or for that matter, their authors. I'm just enjoying the books.

So let's look at the social climbers who can be safely despised, starting with Widmerpool. Of course, Widmerpool is far more than a social climber: but social climbing is an aspect of his approach to life, especially in the volumes two and four of *Dance*.

In BM we find him in tails, fancying himself a standard "spare man" and backbone of the Season. But it's clear that he's nowhere near as successful as Archie Gilbert. We learn later that Widmerpool only ever gets an invitation when a hostess is at her wit's end for a spare man.

Widmerpool has a passion for Barbara Goring, daughter of the peer who used to buy liquid manure from Widmerpool's father -- so it's a passion full of social aspiration, even if it's not quite Mellors and Lady Chatterley. In ALM he is engaged to a different peer's daughter, responding favourably to the urbane teasing of Jenkins, banter that acknowledges Widmerpool's coup in linking himself with the aristocracy.

In CCR we find that Widmerpool has still dizzier aspirations. He's moving in rather elevated circles – "not exactly royal — that's hardly the word yet... You understand me?" It seems he's become an intimate of Mrs Simpson, but alas, the Abdication spoils his hopes of becoming "the Beau Brummel of the new reign". This marks the end Widmerpool's social aspirations: from that point he seeks other routes to power. There is a hint, no more, that Widmerpool's disappointments in society and in love play their part in his shift to the left.

But there's a neat twist to this. Widmerpool is a lord by volume eleven, so in some ways, Widmerpool has climbed to the top of the mountain. True, a recently ennobled Labour peer is not going to strike awe in the Duke of Norfolk. And there is certainly an implication that Widmerpool's peerage is a bit like his famous overcoat: a traditionally ludicrous aspect of everyday life. Widmerpool may think he has won but those who matter know that he hasn't – neither in snobbish terms nor in the deeper aspects of *Dance* in which art and power are forever opposed.

Rex Mottram in *Brideshead* is a Canadian-born millionaire who comes to England demanding only the best. Naturally that includes the best wife, so he makes his alliance with Julia, daughter of Lord Marchmain. He is in business, he's in politics, he's in society, and he's staggeringly successful in everything, apart, that is, from everything that really matters. So he can be despised.

His coarseness, vacuity and inability to understand the sort of thing that we find important is what defines him. Even his good qualities – sorting out the mess when Sebastian is arrested for drink-driving - can be comfortably despised. This prepares the way for one of the most snobbish passages in the history of literature when he and Charles go out to dinner in Paris. Charles chooses, Rex pays.

Not even Ian Fleming has topped this display of restaurant snobbery. Charles orders caviar at the last minute fearing that Rex won't appreciate the glorious "simplicity" of the rest of the meal. "I rejoiced in the Burgundy. It seemed a reminder that the world was an older and better place than Rex knew..." At the end Rex is secretly snobbed for drinking the wrong sort of brandy.

Rex "couldn't see the point of me" Julia says: but Charles of course does. So Rex is triumphantly cuckolded: a conspiracy of two against the hatefulness of a changing world. Whatever Rex does is bad because he lacks a soul. He's not one of us: certainly not what St John Clarke would have called "a natural aristocrat".

In *Lucky Jim* Bertrand proclaims himself an artist, loud, garish and offensive. He snubs Dixon at their first meeting, dismissing his socialist beliefs by crowing about his love of wealthy people who patronise the arts. His girlfriend is a rich man's niece; he is expecting her uncle, Gore-Urquhart, to give him a job; in fact a sinecure that will give him all the time he needs to paint great works. Bertrand creeps to the rich, shows off and scores points against his equals, and behaves dreadfully to those he considers beneath him. Naturally that's mostly Dixon. Bertrand is awful, and to Dixon's intense relief, it turns out that Bertrand is not much cop as a painter.

Three monsters, then. All social climbers. They're not entirely defined by their social climbing, but social climbing is an aspect of their monstrosity. Widmerpool is by far the most subtle of the three, being a leading character who appears in a dozen novels. Rex is a brilliant caricature: we are invited to pity him in a way that makes us slightly smug. Bertrand is a glorious hate-figure: "I happen to like the arts, you sam." (That being his affected and offensive pronunciation of "you see".)

But these despicable social climbers hide, at least in part, the fact that the heroes of the works in which they appear are also social climbers: characters for whom social climbing is nothing less than a noble quest (*noblesse oblige*, as Sillery would say). We are invited to rejoice in their social successes: to see them as fair rewards for life's endeavour.

Like Widmerpool, Jenkins gets engaged to a peer's daughter. Unlike Widmerpool he marries her: and their lifelong happiness is an obscure rebuke to Widmerpool. Jenkins, like Widmerpool, comes from an unglamorous background, but unlike Widmerpool he succeeds in marrying into the nobility. By the end, he's set himself up as a country gent with nice house and enough land to put up a caravan and two horses without worry.

Much of the *Dance* opposes the values of Jenkins and of Widmerpool. (In the war trilogy we can see the value of Widmerpool even as he becomes increasingly unsympathetic.). Sometimes this comes down to a straight contest between the two men. They

41

compete for the affections of Barbara, for the favours of Gipsy, for the hand of a Hon. There is a faint hint that Jenkins's social success is a judgment on Widmerpool: and at the last, there is Jenkins in his big house with his lovely well-connected wife, and there is Widmerpool in an overgrown cottage stuffed full of weirdoes, and not even in charge.

There is a whiff of just desserts in this, a hint of smugness. To make too much of this would be grotesque simplification of a complex work of art, but Jenkins's successful social-climbing does set off the ultimate failure of Widmerpool's life and values.

Social-climbing is a very different matter in *Brideshead*. Charles's passion for an aristocratic family and for the place where they live is portrayed as a yearning for the divine: *Et in arcadia ego* is the title of Book One. Charles' bedazzlement with Sebastian, with the great house, with the entire family, and subsequently with Sebastian's sister Julia reads like a mystic's longing for union with God. The book is subtitled *The Sacred and Profane Memories of Captain Charles Ryder*.

The book is best remembered for its recollections of Arcadian times, so gloriously done that it comes a shook to realise how few pages they take up. Oxford has the barest outline; the summer at Brideshead Castle is also shown with dazzling economy. "If only it could be like this always," says Sebastian. "Always summer, always alone, the fruit always ripe and Aloysius in a good temper." Aloysius being Sebastian's Teddy, of course.

It's not social climbing in any straightforward and bestial sense of the term. Charles still yearns for Brideshead and its family after marrying into the aristocracy, taking Celia, the sister of Viscount "Boy" Mulcaster, as his wife.

But she means nothing. It's Brideshead that Charles longs for and it to Brideshead that he returns, meeting Julia by glorious chance on his voyage home from America. In another bravura passage, the two come together when a storm has prostrated almost everybody else on board: two whole people in a world of the sick.

Julia eventually takes Charles to her bed: and this provides one of the oddest moments of a book not without its oddness. "It was as though a deed of conveyance of her narrow loins had been drawn and sealed. I was making my first entry as a freeholder of a property I would enjoy and develop at leisure."

The two go straight to Brideshead Castle, Charles abandoning wife and children without a backward glance. And so Charles takes ownership, as it were, of Brideshead, at least for a while, and we are invited to share his sense of tragedy – of the meaninglessness of all subsequent life – when things go terribly wrong. Truth, religion, meaning, joy and God Himself are all present under the great dome of the Brideshead Castle: and to be banished from the place for the second time is banishment from Eden.

This is one of the most heroic social-climbs in literature: and the tragedy is not that Charles finds his achievement empty – not in the least – but that it must end. A war and a rotten unfeeling begrudging world must destroy everything that matters.

Jim Dixon is every bit as successful a social climber as Charles, and as with Charles, his social-climbing has elements of a noble quest: for fulfilment, conquest and – above all - revenge. The Bastille of class is well and truly stormed. Dixon starts and finishes much lower than Charles, but he has managed at least as much in terms of vertical ascent.

Jim is out of his depth socially and academically at the university where he is a probationary lecturer. He is dependent on Professor Welch's goodwill for advancement but he loathes Welch and all he stands for. So he creeps and toadies to Welch while fancying himself a martyr for doing so.

Though a little inclined to play the rough diamond and working-class hero, Dixon is a lower-middle-class boy trying to be an upper-middle-class boy. But he reserves his right to despise the upper-middle classes as he does so: it's a kind of win-double.

He also despises all forms of high culture ("filthy Mozart") and believes every attempt to reach it is pretension. He has no interest in history, even though he's a history lecturer. He got the job because he specialised in medieval history – Welch's passion –

but he only did that because the mediaeval course was a soft option when he was an undergraduate.

Like his enemy Bertrand, Jim had designs on the well-connected Christine, even though Margaret, his not-quite girlfriend, tells him frankly that she's out of his class. He behaves appallingly at the Welchs' arty weekend, sneaking off to the pub, getting pissed, topping up with most of a bottle of sherry on his return and then setting his bedroom on fire. His social-climbing looks set for disaster.

But he succeeds where Bertrand failed in ingratiating himself with Gore-Urquhart, Christine's rich and powerful uncle: "I'm the boredom detector. I'm a finely tuned instrument, if only I could get hold of a millionaire I'd be worth a bag of money to him…"

And so, after his disastrous public lecture, one of the great comic set-pieces in literature, he finds that he rather than Bertrand has got the Gore-Urquhart job. Then, after his bus-journey to try and catch Christine at the train station, another great comic set-piece, he finds that he's got the girl as well.

The social climber as hero recreates the ancient Rags to Riches story, in the manner of Cinderella or Jane Eyre or Leicester City. It's an archetypal theme, celebrated in Christopher Booker's exceptional book *The Seven Basic Plots*. Booker lists among many other examples of Rags to Riches, Joseph and his coat of many colours, King Arthur, the ugly duckling, *Great Expectations, Moll Flanders* and

Superman: and we can lob in the more recent Harry Potter, escaping from the cupboard under the stairs in Privet Drive to become the hero who saved the world. We can also add the three works under discussion here.

The theme of social climber as hero is open to legitimate political criticism, for it reinforces rather than questions the social structure: after all, can't be anything wrong with the system if it produces our hero. Amis himself made the transition from post-war Angry to a self-caricaturing right-wing blowhard. But the theme is deeper than politics: it's about the victory of the underdog, and we're all underdogs in an unforgiving world. It's the dream of X Trapnel: to be "immune to the ordinary vengeances of life... beat the book, romp home a winner at a million to one."

Rags to Riches remains a universal theme, but in the English novel this is frequently expressed as social climbing. Nick Jenkins marries an earl's daughter and moves into a house with a drive, Charles Ryder wins, at least for a while, the heart of Brideshead and Jim Dixon has a fancy job in London and a fancy London girlfriend.

Three triumphs. Three heroes. Three social climbers who scale their Everests. Three great novelists who invite readers to share the joy and meaning and power and glory of a successful social ascent.

My Father's Affair With Jean Templer

This is the text I prepared for the APS annual lecture at the Travellers Club in 2023. The actual talk, as heard by the members, was cut down from this to fit the time available, but in the lavish spaces available to me now, I have been able to put those lost jokes back in.

My father was a romantic to the end. He died in 2021, aged 92, still convinced that *A Dance to the Music of Time* was a love story, every page haunted by the narrator's love and loss of Jean: that Nick Jenkins loved Jean Templer in the first volume and he loved her right until the very last chapter of the very last.

My father left school in Wigan at the age of 14, dismissed as a hopeless fool, and he suffered all his life from never-diagnosed dyslexia. He was a very slow reader, but immensely dogged. As a result he was a deeply *serious* reader: he never bothered with anything even remotely trivial: quite literally, he didn't have the time.

This lack of formal education didn't hamper him. He was a very successful juvenile lead in northern theatre and, after national service, he moved into the television in the 1950s, working for many years as producer of *Blue Peter* before establishing such programmes as *Swap Shop, Record Breakers, Grange Hill* and always and especially *Newsround*, for which he won a Bafta for a lifetime achievement.

He was surely the architect of many of the childhoods of today's audience.

I tell you all this because I wouldn't like you to think my father was a fool. I introduced him to the *Dance* and he took to it at once, reading it with immense pleasure over the course of two years or so. I remember his delight in telling that he had been hailed by a titled acquaintance as he crossed Piccadilly near the Ritz: an almost unimprovable Powellian experience.

But he was convinced at a very early stage that among the many characters that move in and out of the novel and of Nick's life, the most important was Jean, and that Nick's unquenchable love for her dictated the course of his life and the nature of his experience.

Well, we all have to accept that everyone's personal understanding of any work of art is valid – you might see a sinister strain in Bob Cratchit, conventionality in Stavrogin, delicacy in Molly Bloom, as Nick remarks to X Trapnel in the course of one of their pub discussions about literature. All the same, Jean's role in the novel has to be set against the marriage of Nick and Isobel Tolland, which is, at least on the face of things, flawlessly happy. More of that later: but rereading the *Dance* – something "not far short of a vice" as Powell remarks in another context – some time after my father's death, I thought it was at least worth giving his view a decent gallop.

For some reason – if I might use that quintessential Powellian phrase – it is clear from Jean's first – highly unpromising – appearance in the work, that she will play an important part in the events that follow. So perhaps we had better look more closely and see if we can find that reason.

For a start, when Nick arrives at the Templers', first-time readers are *waiting* for something to happen. Being used to novels constructed on a more modest scale, we are not yet accustomed to the rhythm of this vastly more ambitious length, and also to the fact that major events aren't necessarily going to happen. So perhaps many readers are keyed up for a big love interest when Jean makes her first appearance – enigmatic, to say the least, to borrow another Powellian locution.

She is fair, not strongly pretty, with long legs and short, untidy hair – Powell found untidiness sexy, and was attracted all his life, as he once remarked, to girls "who look as if they've been dragged through a hedge backwards". She is compared to an old master drawing, Flemish or German, depicting some young and virginal saint, "the tennis racquet, held awkwardly at an angle to her body, suggested at the same time an obscure implement of martyrdom."

Nick experiences a strong attraction "and at the same time an almost paralysing disquiet at her presence". That sense of almost paralysing disquiet stays with Jean for the next 12 volumes: her intermittent presence - and even her prolonged absences - are marked almost invariably by this *almost* – note the Powellian reluctance to commit overwhelmingly to any one emotional state – paralysing disquiet.

She makes one remark: "The hard tennis court needs resurfacing". To have complained about a grass court would have been far too cringing a surrender to gentle manners and friendly vibes. The nature of the tennis-court is as hard as Jean herself seems: we are left with the impression of rather unpleasant and very rich little girl who could do with a bit of resurfacing herself.

Powell takes us through two and half volumes before he gets them in a clinch: and what a shame it is that X Trapnel never gets an opportunity to discuss fiction over the longer course. Of course, Trapnel never had the stamina for such a work himself, but it would have been interesting to hear his views on the technical possibilities, difficulties and opportunities associated with fiction as an ultra-marathon event.

The relationship established between Nick and Jean for the duration of the house-party in QU is not touched on: instead, we are taken with a jump to the Horabins' dance and to Nick's realisation that he was not a success with Jean. "As it happens I cannot even remember the specific incident that clarified, in some quite uncompromising manner, the positive recognition that Jean might prefer someone else's company to my own". This comes after the detail-by-detail scene of Sunny Farebrother's collar-turning machine, and just before an almost equally detailed description of Jimmy Stripling's attempted practical joke against Farebrother.

But we are given only the vaguest outline of Jean's snub, a point where most novelists attempting a *bildungsroman*, would have gone big on the horror of this incident. Perhaps that's because, as Trapnel says of autobiographers, they are imprisoned in their own egotism. But, rather disconcertingly, Powell chucks it away. Nick's feelings are not, it seems, the real issue, not something to probe too deeply - something that it might be rather ill-bred to harp on or even to ask about. It happened, let's leave it at that, and hurry on to the scene after the ball with the chamber-pot and the hat-box. Is it significant that it's Jean who draws attention to Farebrother's luggage, thereby giving Stripling the idea for his jape? Should we see it as a bit of idle cruelty at the expense an established butt of in-house humour? If so, the joke falls flat.

So Nick leaves the Templers' house hopelessly, in both senses of the word, in love, and the reader is inclined to feel reasonably sympathetic, the male reader at least reminded of the dreadful incompetence of one's earliest attempts at love. But there is also the feeling that Nick has had a narrow escape: Jean is rude, cruel, unfriendly, spoilt, unamusing and hard as tennis-courts. Better luck next time, Nick.

But the next chapter begins with Nick's decision - he puts it that way himself – to be in love. "Accordingly, when I used to consider the case of Jean Templer, with whom I had *decided* I was in

51

love..." He thinks of her obsessively as he makes the hot and stressful train journey across France towards the extraordinary household of La Grenadière, where Suzette's physical presence allows her to take priority over memories of Jean, however tender. Later on and back in England, Nick describes Suzette to Stringham but doesn't mention Jean. And then, in the course of the disastrous adventure of Peter Templer's Vauxhall, Nick asks Peter for news of Jean, and hears that she's in love with a married man twice her age. Duport asks: "Is that the sister I'm after?" "That's the one," Peter replies – and the subject is allowed to rest there as they head towards the ditch, destiny, and the sundering of friendships.

By the beginning of the second volume, *A Buyers' Market*, Jean has been, like Suzette, reduced to a dim if desirable memory: and Nick congratulates himself on the maturity of his approach towards Barbara. And so events move on, to the episode of Barbara, Widmerpool and the sugar-castor, and then on further to the louche party given by Milly Andriadis.

This is a bravura piece of plotting, with the events of a single evening sweeping through dinner at the Walpole-Wilsons, the Huntercombes' ball, three chance meetings in the street and Milly's party. Nick, both bewildered and enthralled, eventually finds himself in conversation with a young man with an orchid in his button-hole, which is perhaps a subtle nod at Proust, who was famously painted wearing just such an orchid – a cattleya, naturally. Here he learns that the house was rented from Duport, who is now married. "Now I felt for some reason, inexplicably annoyed that he should own a house like this one, however ineptly decorated, and also be the possessor of a wife whom my informant – whose manner suggested absolute infallibility on such matters – regarded as attractive... this seemed, on examination, a contrast from which I came out rather poorly."

It gets much worse when he learns that the wife in question is Jean. Nick experiences "deep vexation"... and then things move on and Stringham is having a row with Milly and the evening comes at last to an end,

So then Nick finds himself lunching at Stourwater sitting next to a woman unknown to him. She turns out to be Jean, and suddenly the conversation takes off: racy, sexy, intimate. We have all experienced those moments when suddenly a conversation becomes drenched in Tabasco, when some rough magic seems to have taken hold of proceedings. Nick feels "rather breathless" after their initial exchange, and they make a return to banalities. There is feeling at once that the conversation has missed its trajectory.

Already Nick is wondering if he is again in love with Jean. "The truth was that I had become once more aware of that odd sense of *uneasiness* which had assailed me when we first met." He doesn't think there's much he can do about it, not least because Jean is married and therefore beyond his range. She has sneaked away from the company, but turns up again just as Nick and the rest of the party are leaving and suggests: "Come to dinner or something." "I told her my address, feeling at the same time that dinner with the Duports was not exactly the answer to my problem."

So then we move on the third volume, *The Acceptance World*, in which Nick and Jean finally end up in each other's arms. It has taken getting on for 200,000 words to get them there, and it reads seamlessly. But when you have completed the sequence and start to look back, it's clear that this is, if only in purely literary terms, a rather odd business. Nick has already been firmly established as an observer, not a participant. As Powell said himself: "I'm a great admirer of Proust and I know his works very well. But the essential difference is that Proust is an enormously subjective writer who has a peculiar genius for describing how *he* or his narrator feels. Well, I really tell people a minimum of what my narrator feels – just enough to keep the narration going – because I have no talent for that sort of self-revelation."

But in the third volume the central event is Nick's affair with Jean. The observer takes centre stage. Powell has gone to great pains to establish Nick as an ethologist, a student of animal behaviour, noting down the doings that take place within the herd or the pride or the pack, perhaps even refusing to give names to individuals, giving them numbers instead: I read a deeply affecting account of what might have been the perfect wolf; he is always referred to as Twenty-One.

It reminds me of the great David Attenborough series *Life on Earth*, in which the evolution of the animal kingdom is presented with detached wonder – and then, almost at the end, there is Attenborough romping with gorillas, involved quite literally up to his neck.

The affair with Jean begins at last when Mark Members stands Nick up when they have a date at the Ritz, and by chance, or rather by a classic Powellian coincidence, Nick runs into Templer. It's a great reunion, Templer on the very top of his form, filling Nick up with the latest news, including the fact that his sister Jean is living apart from her husband, Bob Duport, with their child Polly. This information fills Nick with "inner dissatisfaction", even though he "hadn't thought of her for ages".

She arrives at the Ritz with Templer's wife Mona, and though she is completely eclipsed by Mona in terms of flamboyant good looks, dramatic presence and relentless conversation, Nick finds himself fully taken up with her, feeling a subtle resentment at her reserve, which is also, of course, a challenge: and once again they engage in "brisk conversation that led in the end to acres of silence."

But something is going on -- and that's when Powell slips the gears of time, one of his more brilliant stylistic tricks: "Afterwards, I could never recall much about that dinner at the Grill, except that the meal conveyed an atmosphere of powerful forces at work beneath the conversation." This leads by easy stages – another useful Powellian phrase – to the

55

journey to the Templer home in the motor-car, when Nick takes Jean in his arms a few hundred yards past the point where the illuminated young lady in a bathing dress diving eternally through the petrol-tainted air.

All this is heady enough, and again recalls, perhaps even deliberately, the moment when Swann at last embraces Odette in the back of the carriage in the course of the first volume of another extended work about Time, after the horses' sudden start has displaced the cattleya orchid in Odette's corsage. And it's here, just past the illuminated lady and right at the start of the long-awaited affair, that time slips another cog and Nick is already looking back at their time together, a time now fabled by the daughters of memory: "I used to wonder afterwards whether, in the last resort, of all the time we spent together, however ecstatic, those few moments in the Great West Road were not the best."

Here we foresee Nick, already sad and disillusioned and half-cynical, in a slightly self-protective way. And then after the mad lunch party with Quiggin, Stripling and Mrs Erdleigh, Jean is playing hard to get: a repeat visit along the corridor that night is not a good idea, she won't come to his flat on Tuesday or that matter, Wednesday. And then what is perhaps the clincher: "You must be discreet... bur really discreet". And yes, she will come to his flat on Friday. In secret.

The level of discretion is entirely in Jean's hands. She opens the door of her flat to him naked, a moment never forgotten "there is, after all, no pleasure like that given by a woman who really wants to see you".. But a terrible quarrel then follows, in the course of which she reveals the – to Nick – utter horror of her affair with Stripling. "I was myself overcome with a horrible feeling of nausea, as if one had suddenly woken from sleep and found oneself chained to a corpse."

This is an amazingly powerful response to something that is not even infidelity. It is perhaps the most emotional piece of writing in the entire sequence, certainly in reference to emotions experienced by Nick. Perhaps it is something to do with vanity: the realisation that Jean sees Nick on the same sort of terms of Stripling: unthinkable to Nick, on the ground of social and intellectual snobbery. This sense of unambiguous horror adds to Jean's mystery: she is capable of half-destroying Nick with a casual word.

Nick later returns to Jean's flat to keep a midnight assignation, agreeing with Stringham that he was indeed "up to no good". He muses on the postcard Jean had sent him, showing two lovers, the woman on the man's knee, above the caption that begins "Sex Appeal". He ponders the awful inevitability of human coupling: "I had enacted such scenes with Jean: Temper with Mona: now Mona was enacting them with Quiggin: Barnby and Umfraville with Anne Stepney: Stringham with her sister Peggy: Peggy now in the arms of her cousin: Uncle Giles very probably with Mrs Erdleigh: Mrs Erdleigh with Jimmy Stripling: Jimmy Stripling, if it came to that, with Jean." After this magnificently Powellian string of eight colons in a single sentence, Nick muses further as he heads towards Rutland Gate, all ready to enact scenes very like those depicted on the postcard. "Darling Nick," Jean says, having told him that her husband is back in England and things might get difficult. "Perhaps, in spite of everything, the couple in the postcard couldn't be dismissed so easily. It was in their world I seemed to find myself."

That is to say, a world in which love that is not million miles away from going through the motions: or going through the emotions: a ritual both damaging and wearying but for some reason essential. At this point, love as a subjective emotion experienced by the narrator, makes a smart retreat from *A Dance to the Music of Time* and, as Nick himself was to do some years later, we start to look at things rather differently.

The whole world, Nick had thought, is the Acceptance World: happiness, he suggests, "is drawn as it were, from an engagement to meet a bill. Sometimes the goods are delivered, even a small profit made; sometimes the goods are not delivered, and disaster follows; sometimes the goods are delivered, but the value of the currency is changed." In what category should we place Nick's affair with Jean? He leaves it up to the reader, being a scrupulously polite sort of author, but perhaps the implication is that it's the third problem that has affected things. The goods were indeed delivered, but the value of the currency had changed. For no very obvious reason, the foundations of the initial transaction turned out to be unreliable, if not fraudulent. Collapse was inevitable.

Another nine volumes remain, and Jean turns up in some form or another in all but one of them. Does the failure of this affair really affect the rest of Nick's life? Does it really haunt the remaining 700,000 words of the Dance?

The immediate post-Jean volume is *At Lady Molly's,* though perhaps my father would suggest that all the remaining nine are post-Jean volumes. It is important for the continuity of the sequence that we get some statement about what's happening with Jean, and Powell supplies it good and early. After some opening thoughts about General and Mrs Conyers and Nick's childhood memories of the dashing Mildred Blaides, he is at work in the film studio, talking to Chips Lovell, and turning down a suggestion that they dine at Foppa's because the place was too strongly reminiscent of his time with Jean. "I was firmly of the opinion that even the smallest trace of nostalgia was better avoided. A bracing future was required, rather than vain regrets." They choose some other restaurant, Nick inwardly congratulating himself on viewing difficult memories in such brisk terms.

He is, then, clearly not "over it" but is keen on the *idea* of being over it, rather than wallowing in it. No doubt all this is familiar emotional territory to most of us, however long a memory it may require.

This resolution, this determination to look at a bracing future, is of course always something you're going to trip up on. We've all been there, I expect, finding some item or some circumstance that has you looking in the rear-view mirror rather than bracingly forward. Nick is inevitably brought up short by Widmerpool, and his unnecessarily lingering account of a lunch in which Jean was present – a meal, moreover, at which it was settled that Jean's husband Duport would travel to South America, and that Jean would be going with him. Widmerpool helped to drive the wedge in between Nick and Jean, and is, at least in Nick's eyes, going on about it rather too much.

Nick muses that Widmerpool couldn't possibly know that anything had "taken place" between himself and Jean – and that is significant, as we will touch on later. But he suggests that "people are aware of things like this without knowing of their own awareness", which is a nice touch. And then he notes that, "conscious or unconscious, Widmerpool had the knack of treading on the corns of others", which adds to our understanding of Widmerpool.

A few pages on, Nick is musing on the subject of Widmerpool, his fiancée Mrs Haycock and love. To Nick, love and Jean were inseparable concepts at one time, but perhaps – perhaps – that's no longer the case. At any rate, he decides that "life could proceed on that assumption". But all the same the thought of Jean reunited – physically reunited – with Duport brings about "a touch of the red hot pincers", along with a vivid recollection of her saying "that was rather a wet kiss". Perhaps this was a throwaway remark *in flagrante*. He is, as he admits, dramatising his own situation by dwelling on sentiment and sensuality: sweet and inviolable things that can never be damaged now they are safely in the past and still unknown to anyone, even Widmerpool.

The events of *At Lady Molly's* lead to a central scene, perhaps the most astonishing in the entire sequence, in its suddenness, and the way it plays merry hell with the conventional notions of linear time in what is, after all – ask Trapnel – a naturalistic novel. That comes when Nick meets Isobel: "Would it be too explicit, too exaggerated, to say that when I set eyes on Isobel Tolland I knew at once that I should marry her?"

This seems at once recklessly romantic, but we are at once brought down to earth by a series of Powellian qualifications. It is as startling a sequence as that with Jean in the back of the motor-car along the Great West Road: in fact the two make a fine antithetical pair. The first is about sensual and sentimental love: the second is about the kind of love that goes right to heart of things, deep, powerful and packed with ineffable meaning. The difference, should it need spelling out, between a lovely love affair and a good marriage.

And then at once Nick is asking, what about Jean? He is still not sure if he is wholly cured. All he can do is leave it at that: what indeed? You can see this as Nick confessing to a pleasant nostalgia for a mad and secret love, or as my father did, a revelation of the fact that Nick never was truly cured: that he never really did get over his love for Jean: that he loved Jean until the last bonfire was lit and the formal measure of the seasons was suspended.

She turns up once more in this volume: Nick meets Peter Templer, Jean's brother, at Dicky Umfraville's night club, and Peter passes on the latest news, including the fact that Jean has left Duport once again, and gone to stay in Rome with Baby Wentworth. "It was quite a good test and I came out of it with flying colours, that is to say, without any immediate desire to buy an air ticket to Rome."

How should we read that? Precisely as Nick states it: he really is over it? Or as Powell implies, that he is making progress but prone to alarming lapses? Or do you prefer my father's view? But time is marching on, Nick and Isobel are to be married and Nick is always welcome to hear Widmerpool's views on marriage. A bracing future is now inevitable, there being no other choice: Jean is probably in Rome, Nick is engaged and time's winged chariot is hurrying on as fast as ever - perhaps even faster.

There is only one mention of Jean in the fifth volume, *Casanova's Chinese Restaurant*. We begin with a flashback: in Hilary Spurling's chronology we move back from 1934 at the end of the previous volume to memories of 1928 or 29, all this by way of an encounter with a bombed-out pub, which must be in the late 40s. In the flashback to the 20s and the early days of Nick's friendship with Moreland, they debate which three women they would chose as wives, were such a thing feasible. Nick adds aside: "Those were the days I loved Jean Duport. Moreland

knew nothing of her, nor did I propose to tell him."
We have just been hearing what great friends they are
– deeply and subtly in sympathy – and yet here is a
plain refusal to confide. We'll leave that there: and
pick it up later because it's perhaps more significant
than it first appears.

There is a great deal of other stuff going on,
but Jean haunts the second chapter of *The Kindly
Ones*, brought to mind by the arrival of Peter Templer.
Isobel appears to have guessed at least something of
Jean's significance in Nick's life. Nick recalls their
parting, infinitely painful, hears of her divorce from
her "awful husband" and then takes his seat in the
dining-room where he and Jean first struck a spark in
front of the tapestry that – suitably enough, as Nick
remarks, a rare excursion into lubriciousness -
represented Lust.

Jean, then is unforgotten. Jean has helped to
make Nick what he is as he stands on the edge of the
Second World War. That paves the way for one of the
great five-star coincidences of the Dance. I have
written at length about the Powellian Coincidence for
Secret Harmonies, and this one is, to borrow an
Americanism, a doozy. Nick runs into Duport at a
boarding-house in an unnamed seaside town that
seems to be Bournemouth, and they go out drinking –
discussing life, love, loss, Widmerpool and Jean.

It is then that Nick learns that he had not, after all,
simply got the better of Duport in the matter of Jean,
as he had always assumed: she had something else
going as well, and that was with Duport's despised

hanger-on Jimmy Brent. Duport says: "Nothing like facing facts when you've been had for a mug in a big way." Nick silently agrees. After this revelation the idyllic past takes new shape: bringing sanity, although sanity might be unwelcome. "I, even more than he, had been made a fool of." The sentimentalised past has been destroyed. It was not, after all, an idyll of love made impossible by outside circumstances: Nick had been a brief source of amusement, subsequently discarded. On top of that, Duport confides: "My wife wasn't really much of a grind."

The episode is matched in the following volume, *The Valley of Bones*, when Nick meets Jimmy Brent, who talks about his own affair with Jean. It becomes clear that Brent is more in love with Duport than he ever was with Duport's wife. Duport is his ideal, a wonderful, intelligent, incomparable man of impeccable taste and judgement. And yet Jean fell for Brent and pursued him, until Brent, it appears, almost reluctantly went along with her. She got back together Duport so that she could go with him to South America and so continue her affair with Brent. And Brent, it seemed was the one who cooled off. "Fact was you were tired of her," Nick says. The past was, then, even worse than it had seemed after the great meeting with Duport. Memories of this fabled time - the naked woman at the door, the rather wet kiss – have to be tempered with the fact that Nick had been made a fool of several times over.

Does that undeniable fact automatically diminish the pangs of remembered love? Does it actually increase them? I suppose it depends on what kind of person, what kind of lover you happen to be. Powell is happy to leave that one hanging in the air, a perpetual reminder of Bertie Wooster's principle: "I'm not absolutely sure of the facts but I rather fancy it's Shakespeare who says that its always just when a fellow is feeling particularly braced with things in general that fate sneaks up behind him with a bit of lead piping." And that is so obviously the case that Jean fails to make the following volume entirely: *The Soldier's Art* is the only Jean-less volume in the Dance.

The action of the ninth volume *The Military Philosophers* comes to a logical conclusion at the victory service in St Paul's Cathedral and, in another five-star coincidence, the meeting with Colonel Flores, who turns out to be Jean's new husband. In order for this to work as effective fiction for new readers, and for that matter, old ones as well, Jean needs to crop up before this climactic scene -- and you can look at this as lingering obsession if you like. Jean is first recalled as Nick accompanies the military attachés to France, first travelling along the Great West Road and the illuminated diver.

And then in the cathedral itself, Nick is transported by memories of Jean, verses he had loved very much at the time when he loved her:

In what ethereal dances
By what eternal streams.

65

He adds: "There were no limits when one was in that state." But perhaps his use of the past tense is significant.

And then he is walking along the Thames after the service with Colonel Flores, who kindly offers him a lift; and there is Jean. Nick finds that she has changed her whole style, complete with a touch of South American accent. He also notes that her daughter, Polly, is prettier than Jean was at the same age, but that Jean's attraction had something more than prettiness. And as they travel towards Knightsbridge, Nick vividly recalls making love with her, and "those very unexpected expressions she was accustomed to cry out aloud at the moment of achievement". But Powell being Powell and Nick being Nick, there are no more details: instead Nick notes that she is now "just short of perfect stranger".

In *Books do Furnish a Room*, Jean invites Nick to a party, to have a look at him and, perhaps more likely, at Isobel. And Nick reflects, perhaps unkindly, that money was, after all, what Jean had always liked best. As they talk, Nick notes that despite the powerful intoxication of the past, he was able to talk to her with "not a split second of emotional tremor". Is that true? Or is this a case of the lady doth protest too much? That's up to the reader. But Nick remembers her telling me "you make me feel so randy" and offers a tease, mild, but one that presumes an unforgotten intimacy: "How well you speak English, Madame Flores."

Jean makes no personal appearance in *Temporary Kings*, but is recalled in connection with Pamela Widmerpool's naked appearance at the Bagshaw house: Jean's naked door-opening really does seem to have been the gift that keeps on giving. And then Nick talks to Jean's daughter Polly, and hears that her husband Carlos is now head of state: that Jean is the wife of a dictator. Nick suggests that she must enjoy being a dictatrix. He is intrigued and amused, apparently unassailed by tender memories.

If Powell had not considered Jean of central importance he would not have put her in the final chapter of the final volume *Hearing Secret Harmonies*. She is recalled, inevitably, when Nick goes to the wedding reception at Stourwater, and then she turns up in person at Barnabas Henderson's gallery, where Mr Deacon's pictures are on show. Her meeting with Nick is without intimacy, and indeed, without even much friendliness on her part, and perhaps on his. They don't even kiss on parting: Jean holds herself too erect to make that feasible. "It was thus avoided without prejudice to good manners". And yet Nick still cannot help but cast his mind back to earlier days: "It's the bedroom, next to yours. Give it half an hour. Don't be too long."

My father saw these passages as irrefragable proof that Nick loved Jean from the second chapter of volume one to the very last chapter of volume 12. It is of course a great deal more nuanced than that, but it's a tenable case. There are two matters arising from this.

The first is that Powell made a very firm decision: Nick's – and by implication, Powell's -- marriage was not to be a subject of the novel, and the character and doings of his wife Isobel were only to be touched on in the lightest possible way; just enough to show that she is great and smart and gorgeous and well-loved.

Powell goes so far as to include an explanation – not far short of an apology – for his refusal even to attempt to portray the marriage. "The difficulties of presenting marriage are inordinate. Its forms are at once so varied, yet so constant, providing a kaleidoscope, the colours of which are always changing, always the same. The moods of a love affair, the contradictions of friendship, the jealousy of business partners, the fellow-feeling of opposed commanders in total war, these are all in their way to be charted. Marriage, partaking of such – and a thousand more – dual antagonisms and participations, defies description."

This self-imposed restraint, coming after the comparatively luxuriant depictions of the affair with Jean, is always going to raise an eyebrow or two. It is perhaps the best solution – I was going to say for a writer of Powell's type, but there aren't any writers of Powell's type, there is just Powell – but like all literary decisions, it has its flaws as well as its virtues. One of these is summed up by Trapnel in his rant about critics.

"How one envies the rich qualities of a reviewer's life. All these things to which the Fleet

Street Jesuses feel superior. Their universal knowledge, exquisite taste, idyllic loves, happy married lives, optimism, scholarship, knowledge of the entire meaning of life, freedom from sexual temptation, simplicity of heart, sympathy with the masses, compassion for the unfortunate..." In other words, as Nick/Powell observes the mess people all around him are making of their relationships in the context of his own apparently perfect marriage, he can look... ever so slightly priggish.

In her superb biography of Powell, Hilary Spurling reports that Powell's wife Violet had an affair during the war. She writes: "She never said who he was, when or where the affair started or how far it got, but she told Sonia Orwell that 'he was the love of her life'. Perhaps he was married like herself, perhaps one or other of them had second thoughts, perhaps the war itself swept them in different directions: at all events, Violet's role as wife and mother exerted in the end a greater pull. Some time later Tony found out what had happened, probably in 1946 when he plunged into a black hole of depression, exhaustion and almost insane overwork."

Perhaps some of these agonies informed Nick's fictional agonies over Jean. And it's certainly true that Powell might have written about this, as trouble between Nick and Isobel, but he chose not to. Instead, the post-war volume, about the rebuilding of British culture, is concerned instead with Trapnel's disastrous affair with Pamela Widmerpool. I don't suppose anyone would want this changed. But in a counter-factual way, it's intriguing to wonder what

69

sort of novel it would have been if Nick's marriage had been under stress, and if Nick had told the story of a functioning and loving relationship that was deeply damaged and yet in the end was re-established, perhaps even stronger and better than before.

Powell chose to take another course – and that's why Nick's love of Jean occupies more paragraphs and occupies more space in the reader's mind than Nick's marriage to Isobel. Powell may not have wanted readers to think that Jean is more important than Isobel, but the way the 12 volumes are constructed, such a conclusion is tempting if not unavoidable. Perhaps the literary moral here is that understatement will only get you so far.

As Nick anticipates his love for Jean in volumes one and two, realises it in three and looks back on it for the other nine, there is much understated play on sensual memories, of kisses and bedding and loving words. But there is another aspect to the affair and that is *all* to do with understatement, with Powell's and with Nick's soul-deep love of restraint, of good-mannered self-effacement – and of downright secrecy. In that flat statement in *Casanova's Chinese Restaurant*, when Nick says that he had no intention *whatsoever* of telling his best friend about his affair with Jean, something else is revealed: the fact that one of the sexiest things about the affair was not just the sex but the secrecy. Nobody knew! Intoxicating thought.

Several times over, Nick stresses the secret nature of their love and his own reluctance to let slip even the smallest clue. He manages not to spill the beans to Duport in their drinking session, or to Brent on the officers' course. Moreland doesn't know, Widmerpool doesn't know, Stringham doesn't know, Templer doesn't know. Isobel has guessed by volume six: testament to her acuteness: in a very polite and self-restrained way, she has got one over her predecessor in love.

But even at the last, that scene in the gallery, Nick or Powell observes that as Nick and Jean meet, nobody could possibly guess that they had been the most passionate of lovers. "There would have been no doubt in the eyes of an onlooker – say Henderson or Chuck – that Jean and I had met before. That was the best you could say for past love." There is, if only briefly, a sense of almost paralysing disquiet – and then she is gone.

And I am reminded of a sequence in one of the excellent Gavin Lyall thrillers, this one called *The Crocus List*, in which Agnes is explaining to Harry Maxim what it's like to operate under cover. "Forget anything you've heard or read about 'living the part'. It can't be done.... Act the part and know you're acting it - and that they don't know. That's really the key. You've got to love the idea, really love it: *they don't know*. Relish it; wallow in it, let it give an extra colour, spice, dimension, to everything you do.... You've got to live in the moment and the way to do that is to think *they don't know* and really enjoy it."

That is at least part of Nick's pleasure: the thrill of infidelity, the terror of being found out, the

71

pleasure of betrayal, of doing something wrong, of keeping a straight face in front of other people, of greeting your beloved with nothing more than politeness when others are watching, shaking hands or offering the faintest of cheek-kisses, knowing the no-good you will get up to next time you are alone. Dylan Thomas describes this in another context: "It was almost as good being a hypocrite as being a liar: it made you warm and shameful."

To have good memories, to maintain a tendrese for a past love is an aspect of the human condition. A lost affair remains preserved in amber, perfect, immune from the tedium and irritations of daily life. A friend of mine, suffering from just such a tendrese, located a lost love through the internet and they met up again – and ran away together, both of them abandoning family life to do so. I asked him how it was going. "Remember now why I left her in the first place."

Certainly Powell is right in that the real nature of a marriage is hard if not impossible to set down in words: the ever-increasing number of years, the minor irritations, the impenetrable code, the shared memories, the small actions, often involving things like cups of tea and biscuits, that have behind them a world and an eternity of meaning, the terrible sadnesses jointly endured, the disappointments, the pangs of nostalgia for life before marriage, the desperate fear that the marriage will end, the acceptances, the absolutely terrible jokes, save that in marriage all jokes are good jokes, the way that a single glance in a crowded room can shut out every other person in the entire universe.

In the end, it's a bit like wildlife documentaries. Even the best and most thoughtful of them tend to bring us wildlife as a series of big-match highlights: instead of sixes and wickets or goals and near-misses it's all kills and copulations. Those of us who spend much time in wild places know that it's not like that at all: these high moments of drama come in the context of hours and days and weeks in which nothing much really happens, and yet you are utterly enthralled. I have, many times, walked the wooded savannahs of the Luangwa Valley in Zambia without doing anything that sounds even remotely exciting to the uninitiated, and certainly without ever being in any immediate danger.

And while such experiences are wonderful to live, they are very hard to tell. By the same token, it is comparatively easy to write about the drama and, for that matter, the copulations involved in a secret love affair, but very hard indeed to write about the endless essential years of marriage in which you never got round to writing anything in your wildlife notebook.

You can say that Powell's refusal to attempt to portray Nick's marriage is a flaw in *A Dance to the Music of Time*, not least because it means that Jean comes across as a more important character than Isobel. And perhaps that's so. In which case we might have to look at the *Dance* as a flawed masterpiece – and then, of course, we must accept that "flawed masterpiece" is the most blatant tautology in all of literature – and that the *Dance* is a masterpiece not just in spite of its flaws but also because of them.

Anthony Powell: Creator Of *Dad's Army*

I first thought of offering this as a spoof. I was going to fake a serious claim for Anthony Powell as the author of the great television sitcom *Dad's Army*. But then I wondered if there was more to the notion than a joke. The film, released earlier this year, brought *Dad's Army* back into the newspapers; it stars Catherine Zeta-Jones, apparently auditioning for the part of Pamela Widmerpool, but that's by the by.

Dad's Army operates on a neat inversion of the stereotype. In traditional British humour, the Walmington-on-Sea platoon would have been lead by the upper-class twit and the one who actually understood what was going on would have been his salt-of-the-earth second-in-command. But Captain Mainwaring is in charge, though always conscious that he is from a lower social class than his number two, Sergeant Wilson.

Mainwaring is pompous, vain, over-fond of authority, self-important, chippy, over-eager to redress the class-imbalance, trapped in a bad marriage, full of unconvincing worldliness, lacking in social graces, ill-at-ease with women, desperate to cut an impressive figure, always eager to get on, and at bottom, mad for power.

Wilson, while always aware of his social advantages, is perennially unprepared for responsibility, seldom gets anything done, is remarkably ineffective in almost everything, but he is charming and at ease in any company. He is quietly successful with women, and has a sound and happy long-term relationship with Mavis Pike. Power interests him very little. He is a man with perspective, balance, detachment.

The Powellian code is not hard to crack here. Mainwaring is an essentially Widmerpudlian figure, while Wilson is like a parody of Nick Jenkins, or if you prefer, of Powell himself; the two even look rather similar; certainly the same air of sadness surrounds them both. One might add to this Powellian resemblance a cast of roughly-drawn rude mechanicals with amusing speech patterns, to be found in the Walmington-on-Sea platoon and in the Other Ranks in VOB.

These slighter resemblances are intriguing, but the antithesis between the two central characters of both works is what matters here. If offered a choice between Mainwaring and Wilson -- or between Widmerpool and Jenkins -- as a companion over a drink or dinner, there is only one choice. But when it comes to winning the war, you might prefer to have Mainwaring, or for that matter, Widmerpool. This is a truth that gives depth to both the sitcom and the novel-sequence.

In a seminal episode, *The Battle of Godfrey's Cottage*, Mainwaring, with Private Frazer and Corporal Jones, goes to Godfrey's cottage to defend the adjacent crossroads against what he believes is the invading German army. His aim is to hold them up for as long as possible before the British army arrives. Mainwaring says: "It'll probably be the end of us but we're ready for that, aren't we, men?" Meanwhile, Wilson is working out how to surrender, in the mistaken belief that the Germans have taken Godfrey's cottage.

Widmerpool wouldn't be worth writing about at Powellian length if there wasn't any point to him. If he was merely loathsome, he would be lucky to last for a chapter. But Widmerpool, like Mainwaring, gets things done. In both *Dance* and *Dad's Army* the man with greater social advantages is generally one-down, and in most practical matters comes off second-best. In AW, Widmerpool's emerging efficacy as a bill-broker is contrasted with Jenkins's startling inability -- his fatalism, his passivity – in the business of the St John Clarke and his never-written introduction to the Art of Horace Isbister.

In the war trilogy, it is clear that Widmerpool is better at winning wars than Jenkins. Widmerpool holds the cabinet offices job for which Powell (rather than Jenkins) was tried and rejected. Widmerpool is a power in the course of the war. If you are going to get involved in a war, then you probably need Widmerpool and Mainwaring rather more than you need people to be charming to local dignitaries or to representatives of foreign powers.

The attitudes of Widmerpool and Jenkins towards the war are made clear in their responses to the Katyn massacre. Jenkins is appalled, though the point, in Powellian fashion is not laboured; Widmerpool is appalled by anyone who wants to make trouble about it. Britain needed the Russians;

Britain did not need the Poles. Humanitarian principles -- perhaps humanity itself -- must be discarded if the war is to be won. And Widmerpool is your man here.

But behind the practicalities of warfare lies the question of what people are fighting for: that is to say, what we will have left when we come to the peace. Jenkins represents the values that must survive the war: art, culture, writing and by implication, love and loyalty, along with all the understated decencies that characterise him. You could argue at a stretch that Wilson represents something of the same thing: civility, gentleness, and a deep if often exasperated affection for his lover, Mavis and their presumed son Frank.

We can only speculate on what Mainwaring does when peace comes to Walmington-on-Sea. But we know what Widmerpool does: if Jenkins loses the war in his life-long competition with Widmerpool, it is clear who loses the peace.

Dad's Army and *Dance* are based on antithetical types: one ambitious, able, power-hungry and unpleasant, the other civilised, decent and rather ineffective. Both types have their points: both their areas of fallibility. Naturally, *Dance* takes it further and goes some way to presenting a resolution. A sit-com can't do that, of course: the situation must be maintained week after week. An ultimate resolution (of the kind shown in the triumphant ending of the film) is by definition impossible.

The nature of the antithesis is actually spelt out for us, in a very unPowellian manner, in a throwaway line from Gibson Delavacquerie: "Love and Literature should rank before Sorcery and Power." So yes, sure - Nick Jenkins and Sergeant Wilson should rank before Kenneth Widmerpool and George Mainwaring. But there are times, plenty of them, when the qualities of Widmerpool and Mainwaring come in handy. And we are seldom squeamish about calling on them.

Withnail And Him

Funny thing, humour.

No doubt many readers will be aware of the film *Withnail and I*. Some will adore it and be able to quote every line; others will resist its delights to the bitter end. It's usually described as a "cult" film: most certainly it continues to divide the crowd to this day.

Like *A Dance to the Music of Time* it's a comedy, and like *Dance,* it's not obviously hilarious. Both operate on the strange – and perhaps essentially English – concept that comedy is not necessarily funny. Like *Withnail, Dance* has something of a cult following: certainly both attract their devotees, and with them, a certain hostility from people who prefer to resist.

Withnail was written and directed by Bruce Robinson (who also wrote the screenplay of *The Killing Fields*) and released in 1987. The plot, such as it is, concerns two out-of-work actors at the end of the 1960s: basically, they go to the country and then they come back. The film is about the end of a friendship, the end of an era and the end of youth. It begins in near darkness -- comedies are traditionally brightly lit -- with one of the characters in the grip of what he believes is a drug overdose.

Withnail and I was made by the company Handmade Films, not least because George Harrison, former Beatle and one of the firm's founders, loved the script. But once production began, it hit trouble. Denis O'Brien from Handmade arrived on set and hated everything that was going on. Robinson said to Richard E Grant, who was playing Withnail: "O'Brien says it's a fucking disaster. It's all too dark, funny as cancer and that you, Grant, should be like Kenneth Williams, throwing your arms in every direction. I told him you were playing a manic alcoholic, in desperate circumstances, and that the comedy was *cumulative*, not Benny Hill laugh-a-minute."

Cumulative. That's a pretty good description of the comedy of *Dance*. Widmerpool's tragicomic end in the last chapter of the last volume is previsioned in Widmerpool's first appearance – poignant and ludicrous - in the first chapter of the first. The scenes are 12 volumes apart and the comedy has a million words in which to accumulate.

Withnail and *Dance* may be comedies, but both are both suffused with sadness. Both end in an elegiac mood: Withnail, a bottle of purloined claret in one hand and a tattered umbrella in the other, recites a *Hamlet* soliloquy to the wolves of in the zoo at Regent's Park ("What a piece of work is a man...") before walking off through the rain to – what is perhaps the end.   (Robinson at one stage considered a final scene of Withnail's suicide.) The *Dance* ends with the bonfire, Widmerpool's death, the suspension of the formal measure of the seasons and the enveloping wintry silence.

There is a scene in the film in which Withnail and his friend ("I", never named in dialogue or in the credits) are drunk and behaving badly in the Penrith Tea Rooms. This was the one scene in which Grant kept corpsing (laughing inadvertently). Kevin Jackson, in his book *Withnail & 1*, says: "Robinson pleaded with him to stifle the laughter, since a major key to the whole film's comedy is that the character should not under any circumstances find themselves amusing."

Here is another parallel with *Dance*. Uncle Giles wouldn't be a successful comic creation if he saw himself as a bit of character, a fun fellow and a something of a chancer. He takes himself with deadly seriousness, and that's why it's funny when he says "I've been having trouble with my teeth" or explains why he never takes tea. Books Bagshaw, Bithel, Erridge, Audrey Maclintick, Mrs Foxe, Mrs Erdleigh: none would be amusing if they saw themselves as founts of mirth.

Most of the humour of the *Dance* is cumulative rather than driving to a punch-line in the classic manner – though Powell uses a punch-line of sorts when appropriate. Example: on the last page of *The Soldier's Art*, after Stringham has been sent to Singapore, Widmerpool has left Nick in the lurch and Biggs has hanged himself. Soper remarks: "In the cricket pav, of all places, and him so fond of the game."

That's funny, but it wouldn't be at all funny if Soper thought it was. It was an artless remark that reveals a half-hearted compassion, along with the need to absorb such shocking events and get on with the job of winning the war.

There are other -- no doubt coincidental – Powellian traces to be found in the film. Withnail himself might easily be a Powell character. He is like Stringham with his wit, style, upper-class hauteur, melancholy and taste for drink: "I demand to have some booze!" He is like X Trapnel in his dress-sense, his flamboyant conversation and his conviction of his own genius: "I'll show the lot of you. I'm gonna be a star!"

Dance and *Withnail* both have oracular characters who give a commentary, half absurd, half significant, on the times they are living through. *Dance* has Mrs Erdleigh, Dr Trelawney and Scorp Murtlock; *Withnail* has Danny the dealer: "London is a country comin' down from its trip. We are 60 days from the enda this decade, and there's gonna be a lotta refugees."

But the important thing that the two works have in common is their conviction that comedy is not a frivolous thing, that comedy can be, perhaps should be more significant than tragedy. The marvellous set-piece of Mrs Foxe's party for Moreland's symphony (CCR) is full of comedy and even has the odd punchline, but while it's going on Moreland is wrecking his marriage and his life, the Maclinticks are having yet another row, one that will eventually end in death, and while Stringham gives a bravura performance – perhaps the last of its kind - it ends as he is chucked out of his own house by his mother's aides, setting off towards his doom with Tuffy in command.

The scene works brilliantly because its comedy is cumulative: at this stage with five volumes to give each nuance added depth and meaning. I suppose it might be mildly amusing to read this chapter on its own; it is *profoundly* amusing to read it – and better still reread it – as part of the sequence.

The scene also works because the characters are not messing about. In his memoir *With Nails* Grant described *Withnail* rehearsals "gnashing at the script trying to get the funny lines to come out of a real situation and *not* sound like we think it's funny." True, Stringham is full of comic stories and one-liners as he entertains his audience, but he is inspired to this detonation of wit because he is making a serious play for Audrey Maclintick, while revelling in this brief freedom from his incarceration at Lady Molly's, where he paints in gouache. Robinson on Withnail: "The comedy comes from character and situation. There are no jokes. *No poncing*."

There is no poncing in either work. They are funny because funny stuff is an inevitable part of the human condition, often most obviously when life it at it most terrible. Both *Withnail* and *Dance* deal with big truths: and both demonstrate the same eternal principle: that comedy is a very serious business.

A Dance To The Music Of Extra Time
Sport In The *Dance*

Anthony Powell once wrote to thank me for all the occasions I had quoted from the *Dance* in the sports pages of *The Times*. Between the lines I sensed a bafflement: that someone clearly familiar with his works should devote a great deal of his professional life to the task of writing about sport. You know, taking sport *seriously*.

Insofar as the *Dance*, or Powell, or Jenkins can be pinned down to any opinion, sport is a bad thing, not worth an instant of an "intelligent" person's time. But it is a truism that the things we find antipathetic are as revealing as the things we hold most dear. It follows that sport plays a larger part in the Dance than you might expect.

The sequence begins and ends with sport, or at least with physical exercise and the quest for victory. One if its two main characters is initially defined by sport. Sport plays a considerable part in the first volume. Sport also provides ones of the book's most striking images.

To sum up the *Dance* in the coarsest possible way, it is about dualities, represented by the eternal opposition of Jenkins and Widmerpool, or rather their opposed approaches to life. This is summed up in a moment of surprisingly unPowellian obviousness by Gibson Delavacquerie in the final volume: "Love and

Literature should rank before Sorcery and Power." That would seem to imply that sport belongs in the second category, as a minor adjunct to the pursuit of power and the repudiation of literature. Jenkins muses on this in the seventh volume, approving a view where there was "no pretence that games were anything but an outlet for power and aggression." There is however, another view of sport: one that both Jenkins and Widmerpool miss.

A Question of Upbringing

The *Dance* begins with sport: with the vision of Widmerpool, returning in the winter mists from a solitary run, training, as we learn, for sporting teams for which he is never selected. It is an image that haunts the entire sequence: Widmerpool's loneliness, determination, oddness, obduracy and strength: his relentless pursuit of power. We are given a very clear visual image: the absurd yet deadly serious figure in jersey and cap, "hobbling unevenly... on the flat heels of spiked running shoes".

Was he really wearing spikes to run along the road? He had previously been running on the ploughed land, we are told, but he clearly has to start and finish his run on a hard surface. Spiked shoes are a positive hindrance in such a venture, damaging to both the shoes and the feet within them. Spikes are no help on ploughed land either.

We are also told that "twin jets of steam drifted out of his nostrils". That is not feasible. When you run, you mouth-breathe from the start. You can run a marathon in a nose-clip without impeding your performance: your need for oxygen, even on a short run – anything that involves the aerobic processes – can't be satisfied by nose-breathing. The two jets of steam are not physically possible... and yet they help to create a powerful and unforgettable image, one that haunts a 12-volume novel. I would like to hear X Trapnel's views on this: an image that is made more effective by means of an unvolitional but inescapable error.

There is also a hint of Widmerpool's ungentlemanly nature here. Training itself was not considered gentlemanly. You were supposed be brilliant without effort: to be born brilliant, rather to acquire brilliance. Skill at sport, like every other good thing, was supposed to be inherited: training was a kind of cheating, an idea beautifully dramatised in the film *Chariots of Fire,* in which Harold Abrahams is even ungentlemanly enough to employ a coach. Widmerpool's insistence on training reveals his lack of class. Perhaps the point is that he makes no attempt to conceal it: sporting ambition is at this stage more important to him than social ambition. When his keenness is praised by Parkinson, the house captain of games, everybody laughs, knowing this is the wrong sort of keenness.

John Powell, an Etonian like his father, has assured me that the football referred to in the text is the field game, one of two codes of football invented at Eton, the other being the Wall Game. The Field Game was compulsory for everyone in the

Michaelmas Half, i.e. autumn term. This involved a good deal of compulsory training, which makes Widmerpool's voluntary extra training not only odd, but fairly fruitless as well. The famous Etonian distinction between rowers and cricketers, Wetbobs and Drybobs, is only active in the Summer Half or term. Jenkins refers to Widmerpool rowing self-punishing "courses" on the river. The detail that he "dragged his rigger through the water" is not a reference to the outrigger, usually referred to in rowing circles just as rigger, in which the oar (or blade) is secured. At Eton the term rigger was (or is) used for the whole boat, a single scull with a sliding seat. Widmerpool is not as shockingly unbalanced as he would have been had his out-rigger been underwater, no matter how ungainly he looks. I should also point out that an Etonian rigger is a better boat than a whiff, which lacks a sliding seat. A rigger is a step up: so Widmerpool was not incompetent. Just not very fast.

John Powell noted that Widmerpool's taste for training would be thoroughly approved of by modern coaches. Modern sport is predicated on the assumption that natural ability needs to be maximised by well-directed training. If Budd, captain of the cricket XI, had trained like Widmerpool, under a coach who had all the right badges, he would unquestionably have been a much better cricketer. That thought is lightly touched on but undeveloped in the text; Widmerpool attempted at school to make up for his shortage in natural ability by hard work and sheer will. That is a valid stance: and it is one he never abandoned no matter what goals he was seeking.

Almost at once Stringham is telling the story of Widmerpool and the banana flung at him by Budd, captain of the cricket team, the first XI no less. It is a complicated issue, revealing Widmerpool's masochism, and his acceptance that there are many ways of finding power, one of which is self-abasement: a theme that will be developed as the sequence of novels continues. We are encouraged to relish the grotesque aspects of the event: and to grasp the power-seeking side of it much later, in a classic Powellian slow-burn.

Stringham's sporting credentials are presented to us pretty early on, with the immediate reference to his pictures of racehorses, Trimalchio and The Pharisee. These at once declare his status, in the world rather than at school: they are pretty impressive pinups to hang up in a schoolroom, and we must assume that they are there to impress, no matter what affection Stringham might feel for them. They are the first fictitious works of art to appear in Dance; neither Trimalchio nor The Pharisee can be found in the stud-book. There are complicated jokes going on here: Trimalchio is a character in *Satyricon*, a work much loved and quoted by X Trapnel ten volumes later; Trimalchio is an ex-slave made good, the ultimate jumped-up individual, and so perhaps a classical Widmerpool prototype. The Pharisees were a hyper-religious sect criticised in the Gospels for their hypocrisy. Hypocrisy and ambition are thus neatly brought into the portrayal of Eton routine, without fuss or bother.

We have a quick run through the sporting CV of Stringham and Templer as they appear, a process that is essential to defining them as schoolboys. We learn that Stringham is not bad at cricket and avoids football whenever possible, which makes him vaguely sympathetic; later that Templer is no great hand at school games "though his build made him good at tennis and golf", which are somewhat suburban pastimes. Templer and Stringham once sneaked off to a race meeting together, an adventure beyond Jenkins's ambitions.

One last sporting note before we leave Eton: Templer informs his friends that their housemaster Le Bas once won the Diamond Sculls at Henley. This is a prestigious event, still contested annually. This detail is part of the picture of a brilliant young man who never fulfils his own and everybody else's hopes: a fine athlete and aspiring poet doomed to become a schoolmaster persecuted by his pupils. Le Bas prepares us for Bill Truscott, an even more promising young man whose glittering career is just beginning to fall short.

*

In the second chapter we are introduced to Buster Foxe, "a polo-playing sailor". Polo is the most thrilling game I have ever played, and it creates obsessives. The sport is also of course notoriously expensive: a trained polo pony, able to stop and turn extravagantly at a mere nudge from the rider, is worth a lot of money and you need a lot of them to participate at a serious level. We learn later, from Dicky Umfraville, how heartlessly Buster behaved, dumping his poor and later suicidal fiancée in favour of Stringham's wealthy mother; perhaps it was Buster's pursuit of the expensive thrills of polo that made a rich wife more than ordinarily attractive to him. Incidentally, Buster is, along with Jimmy Stripling, one of two adults routinely engaged in sport at a relatively serious level. Both are almost universally loathed or despised.

Later in the chapter Jenkins pays his visit to the Templers. Here he has his first sight of his future lover Jean. She is holding a tennis racket as if it were "an obscure implement associated with martyrdom". She remarks enigmatically that the hard tennis court needs resurfacing. Perhaps this sporty introduction indicates that at heart, when all is said and, especially, done, Jean and Nick are fundamentally out of sympathy.

One of the other house guests is Stripling, a racing driver. Let us save him up for the third book, in which he plays a major part, noting only that his skill and daring excite no admiration from Jenkins, even though Sunny Farebrother notes that Stripling "quite often wins those races of his", so he is clearly a decent performer.

We should note that Templer is knocking a golf ball around the morning after his adventure with Gwen McReith, and that Farebrother's extraordinary collection of luggage includes a cricket bat: "A cricketer always makes a good impression".

*

Sports provides the centre-piece of this volume, in the form of the extraordinary tennis match in the park close to the guest-house La Grenadière. Here Widmerpool has already talked to Jenkins about sport; he has little time for it these days "Though once in a way I make a point of going down to Barnes to drive a golf ball into a net." Jenkins is relieved to hear that his self-punishing routine of exercise is over.

The drama of the tennis-match comes from the tension between the serous attitude to the contest that is shared by most of the players, and the ridiculous nature of the court, with its protruding metal framework that marks the lines. Widmerpool grumbles if the game is not taken seriously, while Nick rather enjoys sport played in "these leisurely, at times undoubtedly eccentric conditions". The fact is that all games are ludicrous or none is: sport is about performing a trivial pastime as if it actually mattered.

The tennis-match incident centres on Monsieur Lundquist's tactic of serving "a gentle lob" that catches Monsieur Orn by surprise, twice, in a match involving Jenkins, Widmerpool and the two Scandinavians who are also staying at La Grenadière. Lob? The word can be used informally – you might lob an apple core into the bin. But in tennis a lob is a specific term, and as far as I can establish, always has been: it is a shot that goes over your opponent's head.

A defensive lob gives you time to regroup when hard pressed, an attacking lob defeats an opponent at the net; Andy Murray is a master of that technique.

Monsieur Lundquist's trick serve, then, was not a lob in the tennis sense of the term. So what was it? And why was it deceptive? I suggest that Monsieur Lundquist was serving backhand: throwing the ball up high and shaping to serve above the shoulder, on the forehand, as is conventional, but letting the ball drop below waist height and then dinking it over the net with a backhand flip, stranding poor Monsieur Orn behind the baseline. This serve was routinely employed by Mansour Bahrami when he used to play on the Seniors Tour and delight the crowd with a routine of trick-shots, frequently catching the ball in his pocket as an extra treat. The difficulty of the backhand serve lies in shifting from the fake to the real action while keeping your eyes on the falling ball.

The Lundquist sneak involves us in one of the eternal problems of sport. Sport is played to two sets of rules: one is written and indisputable, the other is unwritten and perpetually re-evaluated. It is legal to run out a batsman who is backing up, but it is considered "not cricket": a shameful action. For Monsieur Orn, Monsieur Lundquist's trick-serve is morally unacceptable. Widmerpool points out that "games are played to be won", but adds stiffly that he too has his standards of behaviour. The idea that sport's function is to teach or to demonstrate moral values was invented in the public schools and remains tenacious.

But Widmerpool's awareness that games are a serious matter gives him a perspicacity that Jenkins cannot rival. That is why he is able to broker a peace between the Scandinavians. The situation is ludicrous, but it is also deadly serious. That's sport for you -- but it is also an essential principle in following the many and varied incidents that follow in volume after volume of the *Dance*.

*

By the time he reaches "the university" (there being only one), Jenkins has left sport behind him without a pang. Sillery declines the opportunity of discussing the college boat to explore the potential of Quiggin; Le Bas turns up unexpectedly and remarks that he rowed in a Duffer's Eight with Parkinson; Parkinson, the former head of games who had praised Widmerpool's keenness. Parkinson failed to get a blue, we learn, scarcely even tried out. A Duffer's Eight is, I suspect, a scratch crew got together for some minor regatta, not an event of deadly seriousness.

A Buyer's Market

Horseracing has few casual followers. People are either perfectly indifferent or utterly absorbed. I recently received a review copy of a book about the greatest racehorse of them all; how many members of the APSoc know this can only refer to Frankel? Fascination with racing is a great bond between people as well as a division: a fact that passed Jenkins by.

94

The second book of the *Dance* begins, like the first, with sport and running. This time the running figures are to be found in a painting by Mr Deacon: the "forest of inverted legs, moving furiously toward their goal in what appeared to be one of the running events at the Olympic Games". Mr Deacon was perhaps more preoccupied with the inadvertent beauty of sport than the eternal quest for victory.

Mr Deacon's art leads us to dinner at the Walpole-Wilsons, and the irrepressible liveliness of Johnny Pardoe. Pardoe is seen at once as a sporty figure as he manages to amuse even the vacuous beauty Margaret Budd by demonstrating a golf shot with a fire iron. In after-dinner conversation he twice brings up the subject of racing, both times gratuitously; it's clearly a subject much on his mind.

He also talks about shooting – but let me make a point here. I am not including "field sports" in this survey; that is to say fox-hunting and shooting. They are not activities in which the object is to find a winner. Hunting and shooting are therefore different from sport, and will be treated as such.

Widmerpool and Jenkins talk, and Jenkins, pleased with his memory, asks Widmerpool if he still goes to Barnes to hit a golf ball into a net. Delightfully, Widmerpool is unimpressed, naturally assuming that Jenkins's thoughts are perpetually occupied with Widmerpool's doings.

The central event of the book takes place at the Huntercombes' ball when Barbara pours sugar over Widmerpool. It is occasioned by Barbara's decision to leave the table at which she is sitting with three men who are all, in different ways, pursuing her. She sets off to talk to Pardoe – about racing. The lure of a racing conversation beats even the pleasure of playing three suitors off against each other. Jenkins had never considered Pardoe as a rival, perhaps because he failed to appreciate the bonding nature of racing. True, there is no other evidence that Barbara was mad on racing – but there would have been no point in talking to Nick on the subject. Racing is a blind spot. (Widmerpool is very much aware that Pardoe, with his talk of racing, is a serious rival.) It's possible that Powell didn't realise that he had created this situation about bonding through racing, bringing in the racing talk for colour, aware only at an unconscious level that the subject divides Jenkins and Barbara as it unites her with Pardoe. But perhaps it reveals him as a conscious craftsman.

At Mrs Andriadis's party, Stringham tells Jenkins that Buster is "much humbled. No longer expects one to remember every individual stroke he made during the polo season." It is a sublime example of a humility beyond the reach of most of us.

We learn during the description of Stringham's wedding that his new father-in-law, Lord Birdgnorth, once owned a horse that "won the Derby at a hundred to seven". Those are unusual odds. I suspect this is a slip for one hundred to eight. If a bookmaker is looking to attract bets on a horse generally offered at 12 to one, he will offer the same horse at 100 to eight, which is half a point better: i.e. 12½ to one rather than 12 to one. The odds of 100 to seven are not mathematically convenient for this kind of bookmaking.

This sort of slip, if it is indeed a slip, would not have occurred in the many passages of the *Dance* that concern business and the metal market. Powell went to considerable lengths to get sound advice; he clearly respected the workings of business. He didn't respect those of sport in the same way, not convinced that sport was worth an intelligent person's time. It's easy to make errors in a subject you don't take seriously; every journalist has learned that the hard way. You don't think that a mistake matters.

However, in the final pages of the book we are treated to one of the great bravura passages in all the *Dance*, and it's about sport. It occurs as Powell discusses Russian billiards, which Jenkins was to play with Jean "when the time came".

Russian billiards, or Russian pyramid (the pyramid describes the way the balls are initially arranged in a triangle) is played on a large table with pockets, narrower than those of a snooker table. It is one of the many table-top games played with a cue. There are 15 white balls and one red. This is clearly not the game referred to here or described in the following volume. It is similar if not identical to the pub game called bar billiards.

Russian billiards was adapted for barroom use. In this new form it was played on a table with a mechanical timer, first in France and Belgium around 1930, where it was called *billiard russe*. A table in England in 1933 (Hilary Spurling's date) was something of an exoticism: quite a coup for Foppa to bring off. The advantage of the game as a barroom sport is that it takes up very little room, since all shots are played from the same spot. Bar billiards was popular in pubs in southern England until the 1970s, when it was supplanted by pool.

Bar billiards is a touch game, one that rewards gentle, accurate and thoughtful shot-making. The balls disappear down holes, each hole worth a certain number of points. The balls are then returned to the player via a chute. There are three pins or skittles on the table: knock a white pin down and you forfeit all the points you have made in that turn, knock a black pin down and you lose everything. The skittle rules might have provided material for a Powellian discourse, but he preferred to concentrate on the way the game is concluded: when the time purchased by the insertion of coin runs out, the baffle falls audibly below the playing surface, and the balls are no longer returned. At this point, Powell explains, all scoring is doubled. This was not a rule in force when I played bar billiards, a period when I was working on local papers in Surrey in the 1970s. I rather wish it had been, it would have added spice; after all, many pub sports have local rules and customs. Jenkins and Jean played their games (when the time came), but before that time Powell reflects on that rule in the glorious final sentence of the volume: "For reasons not always at the time explicable, there are specific occasions when events begin suddenly to take on a significance previously unsuspected, so that, before we really know where we are, life seems to have begun in earnest at least, as we ourselves, scarcely aware that any change has taken place, are careering uncontrollably down the slippery avenues of eternity."

Thus Powell equates life and sport. Both reward the skilful and the lucky, often for reasons that can seem inexplicable, while everyone who takes part finds the activity at the same time amusing, preposterous and quite terrifyingly serious.

The Acceptance World

Jenkins, sitting alone in the Ritz, wonders about making Members a character in a novel. "I found myself unable to consider him without prejudice..." But he then wonders: "Prejudice might prove to be the very element through which to capture and put down unequivocally the otherwise elusive nature of what was of interest."

Within 50 pages Jenkins meets Jimmy Stripling again: a character portrayed almost entirely in terms of prejudice. No one has a good word for him; if they do it is unrecorded and perhaps unnoticed by Jenkins. Stripling is a racing driver, and a pretty successful one. He drives at Brooklands as a wealthy amateur at a time when events there were part of the great summer season of sport, along with Henley, Wimbledon, Lord's and Royal Ascot. In his prime Stripling must have seemed to many a dashing and

99

enviable figure -- and yet he seems almost universally despised. It's as if the whole world shares Jenkins's view.

When he turns up at the Templers house with Mrs Erdleigh, he is much changed from the socially maladroit figure he cuts at the Templer's House in *A Question of Upbringing*. Now he is vague to the point of madness and deeply preoccupied with the occult. Templer gives us a clue: "He had a spill at Brooklands a year or two ago. Being shot out of his car arse-first seems to have affected his brain in some way – though you wouldn't think there was much there to affect."

It seems likely, then, that Stripling has been through a life-changing event, one that probably involved a head injury, perhaps also a near-death experience. But there is no sympathy (or even interest) from Jenkins. Jenkins has no admiration for the courage required in motor-racing (quite considerable, in those days when safety precautions were minimal). Perhaps for Jenkins this is simply the wrong kind of courage: Stripling took no part in the World War One, and Jenkins always has a good word for those who have served with distinction. He goes out of his way to defend Odo Stevens, a plausible and oafish rogue, in the face of considerable opposition: "You must admit that his war record is good". Sporting courage excites no such automatic admiration.

But this dismissal of Stripling as a person of no worth whatsoever leads Jenkins to horror and despair. A little later on, Jean, now his lover, tells him that she and Stripling had also been lovers. It is almost too much for Jenkins to cope with: "as if one had suddenly woken from deep sleep and found oneself chained to a corpse". This is as melodramatic a simile as there is anywhere in the entire cycle. The thought that Jean had shared her naked body – she had a short time ago opened the door to Jenkins in just that state – with such a man as Stripling is almost literally beyond bearing.

But is it really so far-fetched that a girl should go to bed with a dashing racing-driver? Imagine it was Lewis Hamilton or, perhaps better, James Hunt, who seldom had much difficulty in persuading girls to remove their clothes.

Perhaps this prejudice extends beyond Stripling to anyone closely involved in sport – for surely no one involved in sport could be "intelligent". Either way, Jenkins is horribly punished for it. "The pain was intensified by supposing – what was, of course, not possible – that Stripling must appear to her in the same terms that he appeared to me." But he doesn't change his mind about Stripling: only about Jean. It is the beginning of the end, even if a tendresse for her lingers throughout the remaining nine volumes.

With this horror still in the air, Jean and Jenkins got to Foppa's to play Russian billiards, where Jean's prowess is much admired. (It's a delicate, non-macho game.) They meet Barnby and Anne Stepney, who also play: it is notable that the characters play as couples: there is no suggestion of a men's or a women's singles, or a game of mixed doubles. Both couples are out of sorts: "Mrs Erdleigh… would perhaps have warned groups of lovers that the aspects were ominous."

At this point, Dicky Umfraville enters the action. He has been playing cards with Foppa (card games are not considered in this study either; not sport since no physical skill is demanded). He and Foppa have bonded over trotting races: horses, races and gambling make up a powerful force that brings unlikely people together – and leaves Jenkins out. Trotting – or harness racing -- is, as Umfraville says, not a sport much followed in Britain (though I attended a meeting in Prestatyn some years ago). The horses trot or pace (pacing horses move both legs on the same side together; trotting horses move in diagonals) and pull a two-wheeled cart which Jenkins correctly refers to as a sulky, which contains the driver (not jockey).

Sport naturally crops up at the Old Boys Dinner for Le Bas: there is mention of the Test match and of county cricket, details perhaps designed to show how appallingly boring the occasion is and how horribly limited those who take part in it are. Jenkins then talks to Stringham, who is by now recklessly drunk. In the course of his rambling he touches briefly on racing and the time Cypria and Red Eyes dead-heated in the Cesarewitch in 1893 – "or was it 1894? I shall forget my own name next." The Cesarawitch is a late season handicap run over two miles and two furlongs at Newmarket, often with a huge field.

Stringham was right the first time: the dead-heat in question took place in 1893; these horses are real. Back at Stringham's flat the 18th century prints of fictitious horses are still there; he also has a picture of a steeplechase ridden by monkeys mounted on dogs. There are in existence photographs of just such an event, but it is more likely that Stringham's prints were jocular in tone, in the manner of the paintings of dogs playing cards. George van Arden, an American-British painter born 1806, produced a pair: A Monkey Steeplechase and Monkey Cat Hunting, the latter showing mounted monkeys pursing a cat. The works, like the concept, are bizarre, grotesque, funny in one way and cruel in another. Perhaps their quality of recklessness is important to Stringham, and to the reader.

At Lady Molly's

There's not much sport in this volume. Even Widmerpool has given up sport. When he discusses the possibility of a clandestine weekend with his fiancée Mildred Haycock, and Jenkins suggests a golfing resort, Widmerpool says: "I gave up golf. No time." Jenkins, by nature unsympathetic to almost all sporting endeavours, still finds "something impressive in this admission". It is little vignette of Widmerpool enslaved by his own ambition.

Jenkins visits Quiggin – no great sporty figure – in the country. Quiggin is dressed in a zipped woollen garment that make him "look like an instructor in some unusual sport or physical exercise". It's an example of Quiggin's reverse dandyism.

103

Mark Members turns up at Lady Molly's and Ted Jeavons asks him if he plays snooker: a question that appals him. Before the game was made popular by colour television, first with *Pot Black* in 1969, brought to television when David Attenborough was head of BBC2, it was a game more associated with working-men's clubs than the elegant billiards rooms in country houses. Perhaps Jeavons plays at an undistinguished ex-officer's club. It was a doubly preposterous question: that Members should be interested in sport at all, and that he should have haunt seedy clubs.

Finally, when General Conyers is telling the tale of Widmerpool's disastrous night with Mildred, he mentions an acquaintance, Peploe-Gordon, whose marriage was annulled for non-consummation. The General saw him subsequently with another "damned pretty girl" at the yearling sales at Newmarket. This is an occasion at which the wealthy and/or their agents gather annually for the purchase of dreams. I have attended several sales as a reporter, and once stood "in the gate" where the serious players gather and the auctioneer gives you appropriately serious eye-contact. It was as unnerving an experience as I can remember.

Casanova's Chinese Restaurant

They gather -- composer, painter, writer and music critic -- in the eponymous restaurant and they talk: free-associating, boozy talk full of funky ideas and abstruse references. They touch on Casanova, conducting, suicide, seduction, *The Waste Land*, women, time and space, Ernest Dowson, Lot's wife, Don Juan, Byron, power, Andre Lhote, Albert Gleizes and *Henry IV Part One*.

The scene tales place, so Hilary Spurling tells us, in 1928 or 1929. They don't talk about Dixie Dean and the 60 goals he scored for Everton in the 28-29 season; they don't talk about Herbert Sutcliffe's innings on the sticky in Melbourne the same winter. That would be absurd; that would be sport. All the same, the scene came in useful to me when I was covering the Olympic Games of 2000, in which Steve Redgrave won his fifth gold medal at his fifth Olympics. I quoted Moreland's view of Casanova and used it for Redgrave: the reason they were both great was that neither of them got bored.

The spilt between sporty and "intelligent" people is perhaps something to do with modernism: which we might date from 1922, the year in which *The Waste Land* and *Ulysses* were published. It is dramatised in *Brideshead Revisited*, published in 1945 but including a scene set in Oxford in 1923, in which Anthony Blanche reads *The Waste Land* through a megaphone to the people heading to the river to row. Aesthetes v athletes: arties v hearties: if you wanted to define yourself as intellectual, you had to despise sport.

The best theory I have heard for this division comes from Ed Smith, England cricket's national selector, and a polymath. He suggested to me, in a radio programme I once did (it was called *Everything You Think About Sport Is Wrong*) that the issue is narrative. Sport is always a compelling story, that's the point. But modernism is about the rejection of plot: in *The Waste Land*, over the course of more than 400 lines, nothing happens, nothing changes, nothing is resolved, or if so, it is far from obvious. The same holds true of *Ulysses*, in all its quarter-million words. Plot is over, plot is *vieux jeu*. Therefore sport must be the same.

Thus, in this novel full of "intelligent" people, with a set-piece at a party to celebrate the first performance of a symphony, there is, so far as I can trace, only a single reference to sport. This comes, perhaps inevitably, with the appearance of Stringham at the party, drunk but full of brilliant conversation. In the course of his disquisition on marriage, he strays briefly into racing, his mind wandering among "the bookies and Prince Monolulu and the tipster who wears an Old Harrovian tie and who has never given a loser." Prince Monolulu was a tipster and professional character who haunted British races courses from the 1920s to his death in 1965; I can't trace the Harrovian.

The Kindly Ones

The sixth volume begins with the boyhood experiences of Jenkins at Stonehurst, and the intense drama acted out by the servants. After an account of Albert, Jenkins is taken by Bracey, the soldier-servant of Jenkins's father, to a football match at the barracks. It's not clear what code of football is involved; it's all one to Jenkins and Powell. Association football (soccer) seems most likely, though rugby union is a possibility: as a character says in the Gavin Lyall thriller *The Secret Servant*: "Good for morale, to let the troops tear an officer to pieces occasionally." The excursion is a generous action which Jenkins appreciates because it provides an intimate look at army life. "We were still looking at the match, which, to tell the truth, did not entirely hold my attention, since I have never had any taste for watching games". He is "looking at", rather watching the match, which is a delicately-made distinction. I have often written about this phenomenon, this failure to appreciate sport of any kind, and described it as a kind of philistinism. Sport can bring truth, joy, beauty, many other things, and not always in a completely coarse or unsubtle form: failure (or refusal) to appreciate this, on the grounds of intellectual snobbery or simple bewilderment, is a loss, often enough a self-inflicted one. If we are looking for things in common between Jenkins and Widmerpool, we can note that both have rejected games: Jenkins from temperament or choice, Widmerpool (at first embarrassingly keen) by an act of will. Sport was only for him a vector for ambition; when ambition led elsewhere, sport was abandoned.

The book takes us back to running. Dr Trelawney and his disciples participate in slow, non-competitive running, often passing the gates of Stonehurst. This reminds us of Widmerpool's entry into the *Dance*: running and blowing hard. Such exertions are not strictly sport, but they are related to sport. Running is an important act in the *Dance*: it crops up at both the beginning and the end. We will deal with the matter more fully when we get there: stopping only to note that for Dr Trelawney as for

Widmerpool, running is part of an ostentatious quest for self-improvement, behind which there is a quest for power. Both seem to be claiming exceptional, even deferential treatment from everybody else, without having earned the moral right for such a thing.

In the second chapter the narrative shifts from 1914 to 1938; Jenkins learns that the party at the Morelands' country cottage will be travelling to Stourwater in a car owned by Peter Templer. Jenkins sums him up: "Fast cars, loud checks, blondes, golf, all that sort of thing." Golf is included, perhaps rightly, in a list of items that comprise suburban philistine opulence. In *The Acceptance World* there is a similar summary of Templer, this time in narrative: "The women had to be good-looking, the men tolerably proficient at golf and bridge, without making a fetish of those pastimes." Jenkins is prepared to forgive him for these defects, speculating (in *The Acceptance World*) that Templer is "something of a 'spoiled intellectual'". Templer himself points out that he has "rather suburban tastes": adding that "golf, bridge and occasional spot of crumpet" are all he needs to keep him going.

Templer tells Jenkins that he met Buster Foxe at "a golf tournament handicap". In golf, a handicap is not an event. You need a handicap in order to take part in club events: the great charm of the game is supposed to be that players with different levels of abilities can contest a close match (which makes it a decent betting opportunity). But there is no such thing as a golf tournament handicap; a handicap is an event only in racing, shorthand for a race in which the better runners are handicapped by means of additional weight in an attempt to ensure a close finish and a good betting market. Powell has skimped his research on sport again, for the usual reason.

Moreland instinctively dislikes Templer; unable or unwilling understand people who don't take the arts seriously: something of handicap in life. Later on, when Jenkins falls in with Bob Duport after the death of Uncle Giles, Duport aggressively questions him about his interests. Poker? Golf? Jenkins feels rather feeble in his failure to live up to Duport's manly inquisition; it is notable that Duport, later revealed a great opera-lover, doesn't offer music as a possible topic of conversation. But Duport always prefers to look tough: sport, not art must be offered when trying to make an impression.

Powell's friend George Orwell once said that sport is war without the shooting – though shooting is rather a significant matter to keep out of a war. The first half of the sequence comes to an end with the beginning of war: but there will still be the smallest space for sport.

The Valley of Bones

There are people who believe that Powell only writes and is only capable of writing about old Etonians. Such people don't read too closely, and never got as far as this volume. Jenkins joins the army and is swept up into the world of Captain Gwatkin, Lieutenant Kedward and Lieutenant Bithel. Bithel is one of the minor triumphs of the Dance: central to his portrayal is sport and his claim to have played rugby for Wales. It is one of the two great myths he arrives with, the other is that he is brother to Bithel VC from World War One. Bithel, older even than Jenkins, is revealed as a shambolic small-town drinker, fantasist and chancer: rather likeable, so long as you don't have to clear up after him. His impractical nature is borne out by the rugby fantasy. It's a ridiculous piece of deception; it's obvious that he could never have possessed any athletic talent whatsoever. Even Gwatkin says: "And it is my belief, I am telling you, Nick, that all about Bithel's rugger is tommy-rot." This combination of hopelessness and optimism defines him as he continues his pilgrimage through the army: indeed, it seems to sum up the army experience for Jenkins at the time, as if he was part of a nation of Bithels marooned in Ireland with the enemy expected at any moment.

When Jenkins is on leave he meets Dicky Umfraville again, now engaged to Frederica and part of the family. Umfraville gives a brief rundown of his life and wives; racing is an inevitable part of this. His father bred horses for a living: "a precarious vocation and his ways were improvident". But he married money; it's traditionally said that the only way to make a small fortune from horse-dealing is to start off with a large one. Umfraville's second wife, professionally known as Joy Grant "and a very suitable one too", was later married to a jockey called Jo Breen "suspended one year at Cheltenham for pulling Middlemarch", that is to say, preventing his horse from winning. Naturally Umfraville, with his taste for the raffish, stresses that piquant detail of Breen's disgrace, rather than explaining that he (say) won the Gold Cup twice or was champion jockey. (A horse called Middlemarch ran in South Africa earlier this century: a well-named bay gelding by Marchfield out of Romantic Girl. He won once from 21 starts.)

Back at Castlemallock, where Jenkins is stationed ("at Castlemallock I knew despair"), sport is discussed by Jenkin and CSM Cadwallader. Jenkins watches the almost hysterically bored soldiers performing "a Red Indian war dance" and suggests organising a game of football instead. Was he talking about association football (soccer) or rugby union? Certainly rugby is a more serious undertaking than soccer, being a much more violent game. It's easy to play "kickabout" soccer for fun; you can't play rugby in a light-hearted way, so I suspect that is the game in question here. Cadwallader says there isn't another company to play against, so there would be no point in playing. This sets off the only train of thought about sport in the sequence, and the line quoted above: "No pretence that games were anything but an outlet for power and aggression; no stuff about their being enjoyable as such." These bleak, and to my mind rather unsporting thoughts are rounded off by an almost casual flick of Powellian brilliance: "If it came to that, I thought, how few people do anything for its own sake, from making love to practicing the arts."

The Soldier's Art

The central location of this, the second of the war volumes, is a playing field. Here Jenkins oversees the work of the defence platoon when there is a raid.

There is no musing about the relationship between the metaphorical warfare of sport and the real thing as he goes about his duties; either that's too obvious or Jenkins (or Powell) never troubled his head with such matters. All the same, Jenkins must defend what he likes least in his culture. Here he meets Bithel and discusses his baptism of fire and his dud cheques; there, much later, he must go, leaving the drunken Bithel in the hands of Stringham and Widmerpool.

This volume brings us another character who, like Stripling, is almost entirely taken up by sport, and is, if anything, even more objectionable in Nick's eyes. This is Captain Biggs, Sports Officer, Physical Training, one of Jenkins's dining companions in F Mess. Biggs is equally obnoxious in good mood and bad, either grousing or joylessly ragging his mess-mates, especially Captain Soper, the catering officer. Biggs, organiser of sports at a seaside resort in peacetime, is divorcing his wife; he is convinced that the load he has to bear is a good deal heavier than anybody else's. He persecutes Stringham, who turns up unexpectedly as mess waiter, a policy that alienates any sympathy a reader might feel for him. Nick is having a pretty rotten time in this volume; the depiction of Biggs, shown without a single redeeming quality, is the nearest Powell gets to that most saleable (in Jenkins's view) of all qualities in a novelist, self-pity. But if Jenkins is close to despair, Biggs finds the real thing and hangs himself, so that the volume ends as it (almost) began, on the sports field. Soper gives both Biggs and the volume the unforgettable valediction: "In the cricket pav, of all places, and him so fond of the game."

The Military Philosophers

There is not much sport in this volume. Widmerpool, when discussing Polish generals in committee, points out that General Anders once ran a racing stable: "I'm no enemy to a bit of dash, I like it." It forms part of a brief vignette showing Widmerpool's self-confidence and mastery of detail.

Sunny Farebrother tells Jenkins that he ran into Jimmy Stripling in Aldershot, where he was lecturing to the troops about the early days of motor-racing; Farebrother casually referring to him as a "dreadful fellow". Life is tough for sports-lovers in the pages of the *Dance*.

Perhaps it's toughest of all for Captain Biggs, remembered by Jenkins in the course of the victory service at St Paul's: "Biggs, hanging by the neck until he was dead in that pokey little cricket pavilion; another war casualty, so far as that went."

Books do Furnish a Room

Not much sport in this volume either, but a faint whiff of racing pervades it, and eventually provides the pay-off. Racing is just about acceptable in the *Dance* – and here I would like to employ a classic Powellian locution and say "for some reason", were it not for the fact that the reason is bleeding obvious. Racing is a routine preoccupation of the upper classes: for Powell/Jenkins it is socially if not intellectually acceptable. General Conyers, much admired, is involved in racing at its most polite;

Dicky Umfraville, much liked, with its more raffish side.

So when Jenkins is seeking to describe Bagshaw's fascination with far-left politics even in disillusionment, he compares him to a long-lapsed racing man who no longer bets, but still loves talking about the sport. Incidentally, Powell says that this hypothetical racing man has "ceased to lay a bet". A bookie lays (accepts) a bet; a punter places a bet. The situation has becomes more involved with online betting exchanges, but that is not a concern of this volume. It's a small error: Powell didn't get this or any other volume checked by an enthusiast for sport.

In a long and vivid account of X Trapnel and his ways, we learn about the irrational hope that Trapnel "will prove immune to the ordinary vengeances of life... beat the book, romp home a winner at a million to one." Here the unrealistic odds are perfect for the job. This racing metaphor gains added meaning when we learn that Trapnel's father was not, as his son usually hinted, connected with the secret service, but was a quite reasonably successful jockey. Trapnel, described as "well over six feet" must have had a very different build from his father, but such genetic anomalies are frequent enough. But why did he hush up his paternity? Is it that secret service is more glamorous? Is it intellectually unacceptable to have a jockey as a father? Bagshaw says: "He's not exactly ashamed. Rather proud in a way. All the same, it doesn't quite fit in with his own picture of himself."

Dicky Umfraville delivers the pay-off line when asked if he has heard of the jockey Trapnel. "Heard of him, old boy? When I was in Cairo in the 'twenties, I won a packet on a French horse he rode called Amour Piquant." It's a small but finely made example of virtuoso novelistic brilliance.

Temporary Kings

A good deal of this volume operates on the tension between the two Americans, Louis Glober and Russell Gwinnet: their different hopes as regards Pamela and their different ambitions of becoming a complete man. In a rundown of Gwinnett's many qualities, Emily Brightman notes that "he is good at such sports as racquets, skating, skiing."

Soon after this we learn that Glober has come to Venice from the German Grand Prix of motor racing. Spurling dates the Venice events to 1958; in that year the German Grand Prix was held on August 3. Hurrah! A sporting detail spot on. We also learn that Glober is "a noted rider, shot, golfer, yachtsman or whatever else was required by the context." These details set the context for their rivalry. Both seek drama in their lives: sport is an obvious way to find it.

At the beginning of the volume we learn that from Umfraville that "there hasn't been a good laugh since that horse-box backed over Buster Foxe at Lingfield", an accident that was the end of Buster. More racing: when Jenkins asks Bagshaw why anyone should choose to be a crypto-communist, Bagshaw finds his naiveté almost incomprehensible:

115

"like asking Umfraville why he should be interested in one horse moving faster than another, a football fan the significance of kicking an inflated bladder between two posts". Is Nick mocking his own lack of understanding here? Or is he quite complacent about it?

A little later we are treated to the great set-piece of the end of X Trapnel, brilliantly withheld from the previous volume. Such self-restraint, such delayed effects are part of the enduring strength of the *Dance*. This final binge was made possible by Trapnel's acquisition of £100 in cash: possibly a legacy from someone who had backed a winner ridden by Trapnel's father many years earlier.

Ada tells Jenkins of a curious sporting incident at the Palazzo Bragadin. In an attempt to break the tension caused by Pamela's line of dirty talk, with both Widmerpools present, Glober persuades a fellow-guest to teach him cricket, and uses a renaissance mace as a bat. "The maharaja bowled a peach, Glober hit it so hard he caught Kenneth on the jaw." Here is a pleasingly grotesque incident, once again involving Widmerpool with cricketers and flying fruit. Widmerpool gets a real hammering in this volume: as we recollect his youthful encounter with a banana, we have to wonder if that is not, after all, what he likes.

We hear of Glober's death, and it is appropriately dramatic and sporting: he dies in a high-speed traffic accident, the car driven by a racing driver. Glober, in his capacity as "playboy-tycoon", has consistently sought both drama and competition. Sport routinely supplies both, though it also about the pursuit of excellence. Perhaps that's the attraction for Gwinnett, who escapes from all the confrontations to become a water-skiing instructor. Not everyone can turn from academia to sport with such facility.

Towards the end of the novel there is a lot of reference to vintage cars. The world of vintage cars is not precisely sport; is it is more, as Striping admits, a way of enjoying sport when you're too old for sport (rather like golf). The slow progress of the cars is a throwback to Widmerpool's run at the start of the sequence, and a throw-forward to his nocturnal run at the end. Vintage cars create a bizarre background to the last few pages of the book, which ends with a vintage car rally crossing Westminster Bridge. Perhaps that procession sums up the 12-volume sequence of the *Dance*: you can't outrun the past, no matter how hard you try: so perhaps the best way to deal with it is to cherish it.

Hearing Secret Harmonies

There are a few sporting references in this volume. Sonny Farebrother talks of Jimmy Stripling's funeral and his racing career is mentioned, but what matters here is Stripling's apparent association with Scorpio Murtlock. X. Trapnel's final spill was "worse than any on the racecourse" by his jockey father. When Gwinnett turns up at the Magnus Donners Prize Dinner, he could be mistaken for "a retired lightweight boxer or karate instructor".

117

The sports ground at Stourwater is rather carefully delineated, preparing the scene for the arrival of the running members of the Murtlock's cult, and after that, but Murtlock's own rather terrifying appearance. As Nick and Isobel arrive there is a scrap of conversation, not attributed to any character:

"What games would they be?"
"Net-ball, hockey, I suppose."

Netball is unlikely: the game is played on a hard court, not a grass field. Lacrosse is an unmentioned possibility. Later Fiona looks at the playing-field and remarks: "I used to long to die, playing hockey on winter afternoons." Gwinnet, now her husband, talks about the Mesoamerican ball game, which was played by the Aztecs among others. He brings in an appropriately sinister mention of human sacrifice as the runners approach, led by Widmerpool – who is shortly to become a sort of human sacrifice himself. The sequence closes as Murtlock escorts the drunken Bithel back across the playing field, not once offering physical assistance.

The final chapter brings us the last set-piece of the novel-sequence. This is Bithel's narration of the Widmerpool's death. Widmerpool runs out of the novel as he ran into it, fruitlessly seeking advantage, doing so by fundamentally misunderstanding the activity he is taking part in. His last words, heard after he had vanished round a bend in the path through the wood, are: "I'm leading, I'm leading now."

You could, I suppose interpret that as Widmerpool's misunderstanding of the ritual: wrongly thinking it is a sporting event. But Widmerpool also misunderstands sport. Of course sport is about competition and trying to beat the rest, as Jenkins reflects in *The Valley of Bones*. But that is a pretty coarse understanding. Sport is also a quest for excellence: for perfection. It's about the attempt to go beyond human limits. To seek and find a relative excellence in yourself is not a small matter, even in the trivial pursuit of sport. When the great performers find excellence of the highest and rarest kind, there is something marvellous to be found by anyone who cares to look for it.

Ayrton Senna, three times world motor racing champion, who died on the track in 1994, spoke the following word to me besides the racetrack in Montreal: "Every time I have an idea about where my limits are, I go back to check it. And most of the time I am wrong. So I have to adjust myself to going even further…"

Was Widmerpool An Acidhead?

Some people find the last volume of *Dance* the least satisfactory. They say Powell never understood the 60s, that Scorpio Murtlock – or at least the power he exerts – is not entirely believable, and that Widmerpool's descent into madness is inconsistent with the previous 11 volumes. It doesn't seem that way to me. Perhaps that's because I was there. In the High Sixties, I mean.

A good friend of mine, an aspiring poet of some talent, fell for – in both senses – a self-styled spiritual leader. His collapse into madness haunts me still. I have laughed through the night with a head full of hash; I had a beatific experience with a hammock, a hoverfly and LSD; I hitched round Europe sleeping in parks and ditches; I listened to the Incredible String Band and I read all the hippy set texts, a number of which – *The Prophet, The Teachings of Don Juan, Steppenwolf* – had characters who reveal the true wisdom of the universe.

So I am qualified to make certain judgments about Powell's depiction of the Hippy Era -- and I can say with confidence that a great deal of it stands up. If there is a gap it's in Powell's ignorance of psychedelic drugs, but it's a handicap he mostly rises above – even though the Hippy Era itself can't be grasped without an understanding of LSD. Without naming the drug Powell seems to have understood its importance in hippy culture.

Taking LSD wasn't about pleasure. Acid was a duty: a sacrament: a portal to enlightenment: a six-lane motorway that led to Truth. The LSD experience made artists and seers of us all: it was the democratisation of wisdom. Objective and subjective truth became inextricable and one sense merged with another – the Nobel Laureate Bob Dylan wrote of sheltering from a thunderstorm in a church porch: "And we gazed out on the chimes of freedom flashin'."

We jested that reality was a cop-out for people who couldn't handle drugs. Blake wrote: "If the doors of perception were cleansed everything would appear to man as it is: infinite." For a quid you could buy 500 micrograms of door-cleanser.

And then the casualties started to mount up. Some of those who sought the ego-death of LSD succeeded too well and lost their ability to cope with the world. As Danny the dealer said in the film *Withnail and I*: "London is a country coming down from its trip. We're sixty days from the enda this decade and there's gonna be a lot of refugees." By my reckoning the High Sixties lasted from 1967 to 1972. It was the time of LSD: the Acid Years. Hilary Spurling dates the action in HSH as 1968-71.

The volume begins with the visit of Murtlock and three followers. For me, Murtlock is a reasonably familiar type: a hippy guru with the classic contradiction of bogosity and conviction. Jenkins scoffs about "the familiar ring of Shortcuts to the Infinite, Wisdom of the East, Analects of the Sages."

121

But he is forced to accept that there is more to Murtlock than a few borrowed phrases and "more than mere calculating ambition". As Murtlock hears about the Devil's Fingers "Forces perhaps stronger than himself dominating him, made it possible for him also to dominate by the strength of his own feelings."

This was a time when many people, having rejected the traditional leaders, looked for new ones. These included co-opted leaders like Kahlil Gibran, Blake, Dylan, RD Laing, Jack Kerouac, and Aldous Huxley. And there were plenty of others volunteering themselves: Maharishi Mahesh Yogi, Guru Maharaj Ji, Sri Chiminoy, Carlos Castaneda, Richard Bach, Ken Kesey, Timothy Leary. This is the company Widmerpool seeks to join.

In the second chapter of HSH Jenkins looks back to Widmerpool's withdrawal to the United States, working at "an Ivy League university". In precisely this period Leary was working at Harvard, an Ivy League university. His work there included the Concord Prison Experiment, in which he claimed that prisoners vowed to reform their lives after taking guided LSD trips. He also said that LSD "cured" homosexuality. He took the drug himself and encouraged (or pressured) his students to do the same. The project was closed down and he was fired in 1963. He then became a proselytiser for LSD, coining the phrase "turn on, tune in, drop out". His book, *The Politics of Ecstasy*, was one of the set texts. President Richard Nixon described Leary as "the most dangerous man in America".

It is then, inconceivable that Widmerpool was unaware of LSD. He then goes, we are told to "a noted Californian centre for political research". If Widmerpool was a historical rather than a fictional character, we would assume that he was introduced to LSD in those years. After his return, and his adventure of the paint-throwing Quiggin twins, Delavacqerie tells Nick that Widmerpool "is not far from making himself into a Holy Man these days."

The crucial event in the formation of the High Sixties was the divorce of the hippies from political involvement. The early part of the decade was dominated, at least in the public eye by Vietnam marches, student sit-ins and of course, *les évènements* in Paris, when, in May 1968, student protesters and the trade unions formed an alliance that brought the country close to revolution.

The Hippy Movement rejected violence and confrontation. The idea was to change society by becoming better people, with deeper values: to form an alternative society based on love and peace. The revolution was to take place not on the streets, but in the mind. A changed awareness through the use of psychedelic drugs was an irrefragable (good Powellian word) part of that.

Powell understood this shift from one kind of revolution to another and made it central to the last volume of *Dance*. It is a point that Kingsley Amis, 17 years younger, missed entirely. In *Girl, 20*, his own book about the High Sixties, his hero, the conductor Sir Roy Vandervane, teams up with a rock band called

Pigs Out. That's quite funny: but rock music was decisively distanced from social protest until the Punk Movement of the subsequent decade. Amis got it wrong; Powell didn't.

During the first two-thirds of HSH Widmerpool is an advocate of violent revolution: of attacking society by direct confrontation. At the Donners-Brebner dinner he makes a speech entirely negative in tone: "the wrongness of money" etc. He advocates nothing except rebellion and is reinforced by the nihilistic prank of the Quiggin twins. At this point it is destruction that fascinates him. At the Royal Academy dinner he explains that he is seeking out Murtlock because he is "a vehicle for dissent". Widmerpool also expresses his distaste for "mumbo-jumbo". He gets a stern warning about this and about Murtlock from Canon Fenneau, but proceeds anyway. He wants to use Murtlock as a destructive force.

The next we hear of Widmerpool is Gwinnet's report of the events of the Devil's Fingers. This is a huge leap. Widmerpool is no longer working towards dissent. He is seeking conformity – but to a new set of beliefs. He wants to conform to harmony, and to the thrilling ragbag of doctrines associated with Trelawneyism as interpreted by Murtlock.

Revolution in the mind required a new kind of certainty. Trelawney supplied this in fiction: in real life, Aleister Crowley, one of the models for Trelawney, did the same thing for a number of people. The band Led Zeppelin based part of their album *Led Zeppelin 3* around Crowley; the second side is entitled

124

Do What Thou Wilt, from Crowley's most famous statement "Do what thou wilt shall be the whole of the law". Jimmy Page, the guitarist, bought Crowley's former dwelling Boleskine House.

By the time Widmerpool appears at the Cutts wedding, he is radically changed. He is a total convert to the pursuit of harmony. He is a hippy seeking not to destroy society but to make a better one: and in the course of this quest his personality has collapsed. As the book moves towards its conclusion we get hints as to how this happened: a fight with Murtlock at the Devil's Fingers, in which he is wounded with a knife, the arrival of Bithel, the penances he was forced to undergo to atone for his treatment of Bithel in the army. To my mind these are wholly believable - if Widmerpool took LSD.

Did Widmerpool take acid? I am aware that this is straying towards the question of how many children had Lady Macbeth, but I think it's worth considering. Barnabas Henderson discusses the prohibitions of life under Murtlock in the last pages of the book. Murtlock, we learn, makes no objection to Bithel's occasional drinking: "He'd never have stood it from anyone else, unless strictly for ritual purposes. That was permitted, like getting high on whatever Scorp might sometimes decide to produce." If Murtlock produced drugs, he presumably produced LSD. It's inconceivable that he didn't. If you wish to offer ecstatic experiences and at the same time establish domination, LSD is your drug of choice. Charles Manson used LSD to establish his own cult, the Manson Family, which was involved in nine murders.

The hold Murtlock has over his followers, especially Widmerpool, and Widmerpool's breakdown are easily explicable once LSD is accepted. The effects of taking LSD have been described as "playing Russian roulette with one's mind". The more often you play the fewer empty chambers you find.

Widmerpool's desperate state at the Cutts wedding seems more symptomatic of an acid casualty than someone who has overdone the penance. This domination of Widmerpool by Murtlock is dated by Henderson to Bithel's arrival, an event that gives Murtlock psychological ascendency. But Widmerpool, used to dealing with Donners Brebner rivals, the War Cabinet, Balkan statesmen and many others, surely could not have been nagged into collapse without help. That kind of help is available in the devastating drug LSD. Many great and glorious things came out of the Hippy Movement and the High Sixties: but at very considerable cost.

LSD makes Murtlock's domination and Widmerpool's collapse entirely plausible. I don't suppose Powell knew any more about LSD than what he read in the *Daily Telegraph*, but he has given us a convincing account of an acid casualty. So how did he know? Widmerpool treads heavily on Jenkins's corns when discussing Jean Templer in ALM, though he has no idea of what had happened between them. Powell writes: "People are aware of things... within themselves without knowing of their own awareness."

126

A Great Deal Of Time

A review of *A Dance to Lost Time: Marcel Proust and Anthony Powell* **by Patrick Alexander**

I was banished. Exiled in Dorking. The new chief reporter of the Surrey Mirror, never a great fan, sent me to the *Dorking Advertiser*, where I mostly covered the magistrates' court. This involved a twice-daily 90-minute commute, an hour's solitary lunch-break and plenty of downtime in court.

But never an instant did time – perhaps I should say Time – hang heavy on my hands, because that's when I first read Proust. By the Time my eight-week stay was over, I was already on my second journey through the budding grove with the *jeunes filles en fleur*.

I first read *A la recherche du temps perdu* in the translation by CK Scott Moncrieff (you know how Proust suffers in the original) which came in 12 volumes – and I was high as kite throughout. I hadn't known it was possible to write that that, think like that, see the world like that: so I read the endless spiralling sentences and my heart and my mind spiralled with them. For me, Dorking will always be a town of romance, mystery and profundity, its boulevards and faubourgs thronged with Gilberte, Albertine, Charlus and Saint-Loup, haunted by music and the little phrase of the composer M. Vinteuil.

So when I became aware of another 12-volume novel sequence with Time in the title I was inclined to resentment. How dare this Powell chap come up with such a thing? Scott Moncrieff called the work *Remembrance of Things Past*, referencing one of Shakespeare's sonnets and annoying Proust very much. Subsequent translators have preferred the less fanciful *In Search of Lost Time*.

And here was *A Dance to the Music of Time*, and to begin with I was very much against it – until I actually started reading the damn thing. Then Powell won me over, and that was that. I rejoiced in his subtle repayment of his debt to Proust, first with the Proust pastiche in MP, and then with the visit to Cabourg, Proust's Balbec, later in the same volume.

Patrick Alexander has written a book that compares and contrasts the two big works, and *A Dance to Lost Time* is a damn good read for anyone who has a taste for both of them. The book increases your understanding of both works, and shows how pleasure in each is enhanced by knowledge of the other.

The similarities are considerable: both take on a series of characters who perform against a timespan unavailable to most novelists. Both are set in the real world, in which real events – most obviously war, while Proust has the Dreyfus affair and Powell the Abdication – take place in the background.

Both novelists have a fascination with the aristocracy, both come from privileged backgrounds, both are social climbers. Both, above all, are concerned with the way that Time operates on individuals and on their relationships with others.

But there is one fundamental difference, one that makes these two works utterly different. Powell strives for objectivity: he is an observer, an ethologist studying the dynamics of the herd and the individuals within it. Proust writes, more than anything else, about his own interior world.

Alexander quotes Powell: "I'm a great admirer of Proust and I know his works very well. But the essential difference is that Proust is an enormously subjective writer who has a peculiar genius for describing how he or his narrator feels. Well, I really tell people a minimum of what my narrator feels – just enough to keep the narration going – because I have no talent for that sort of self-revelation."

Alexander also points out another important difference: "Unlike Powell, who sought always to find the different traits that made each individual unique, Proust sought those traits that they had in common and made them a 'type'." For example, Proust has a single character who is a writer – *the* writer -- in Bergotte, while Powell has St John Clark, X. Trapnel, Mark Members, J.G. Quiggin, Ada Leintwardine and a good few others.

Both Proust and Powell have very distinctive styles when it comes to putting the words on the page. By the time he began the *Dance*, Powell had abandoned the clipped Hemmingway-influenced narration of *Afternoon Men*, and become comparatively lush, with occasional convoluted sentences and elaborate phraseology: "To enter Sillery's sitting-room after twenty years was to drive a relatively deep fissure through variegated seams of time."

But every time any other writer goes for lush, Proust gets royalties. Try this, a scene set at the hotel in Balbec/Cabourg where Nick Jenkins regretted he had not spent the night, and from the Scott Moncrieff translation: "Left by myself, I was simply hanging about in front of the Grand Hotel until it was time for me to join my grandmother, when, still almost at the far end of the paved "front" along which they projected in a discordant spot of colour, I saw coming towards me five or six young girls, as different in appearance and manner from all the people whom one was accustomed to see at Balbec as could have been, landed there none knew whence, a flight of gulls which performed with measured steps upon the sand – the dawdlers using their wings to overtake the rest – a movement the purpose of which seems as obscure to the human bathers, whom they do not appear to see, as it is clearly determined in their own birdish minds."

When, still a trainee, I was doing my block release course on journalism, we were introduced to something called the Fog Index. We were required to take a sample of our own prose, count the words, the full stops and the words of more than three syllables and make a computation that gave us our Fog Index: an objective assessment of the clarity of our writing. Tabloid writers, we were told, should aim for eight, broadsheet writers for 12.

I made the same calculation of a chunk from the volume of Proust I happened to be reading at the time. Proust, I established, had a Fog Index of 56. Our tutor told me that was impossible; I told him that the entire page – one long passage of perhaps 500 words -- was a single polysyllabic sentence.

Alexander looks at other similarities and differences. He examines monsters, comparing Charlus with Widmerpool, Pamela with Mme Verdurin. He does the same thing with the "Golden Boys", comparing Stringham with Saint-Loup, and throwing in Sebastian Flyte (from *Brideshead Revisited*) for good measure.

One of the stranger differences about the two works is their attitude to homosexuality. Powell makes no judgment whatsoever: Mr Deacon, Norman Chandler, Hugo Tolland, Barnabas Henderson, Nora Tolland, Eleanor Walpole Wilson, other bisexual characters, are presented without prejudice: some with decided affection.

The later volumes of Proust's work are obsessed with homosexuality and the consequent depravity of characters with a taste for "inversion". And there are more and more and more of them: by the end, it seems, as Alexander points out "almost all of Proust's male characters, with the exception of Marcel, eventually turn out to be gay." And yet Powell was unambiguously heterosexual, while Proust was homosexual (though perhaps not active).

Marcel (as the narrator of the novel) is obsessed with his love for Albertine, who was, of course, modelled on his chauffeur, Alfred Agostinelli. You can argue that this is the great flaw of *In Search of Lost Time*: saying "she" when you mean "he" doesn't automatically make the portrayed relationship convincing. A secret relationship that would, if discovered, lead to disgrace and perhaps imprisonment is not the same as relationship that, if discovered, would lead to a nudge and a wink.

This is a fascinating comparison, one that could happily be taken a good deal further. Alexander has done a good job with it and I recommend it to all Prousto-Powellians. But in all good faith I must do a little carping as well.

This would appear to be a self-published work and good on him for taking the risk: it's a good book and after all, Proust paid for the publication of this first volume of *In Search of Lost Time*. But the lack of editing – the lack of different pairs of eyes to scan the text – has led to a fair old sequences of ouches.

Examples: Gilberte frequently loses her final E and changes sex, characters from the *Dance* include Mathilda, Barnaby and Mildred Blaine, while Peter and Jean are Templer or Templar according to the author's mood at the time. There are also a number of repetitions; in one instance the same 50 word quote appears on successive pages.

But we must do our best to rise above such irritations, savour the similarities and the differences in Proust and Powell that are revealed to us, and then, best of all, feel inspired to turn back to the originals again.

An Evening At Wimbledon Dogs

It is possible that some members of the APS never went to Wimbledon dog-track in the 1970s. That was, of course, before they sanded the bends, and on rainy nights, if you backed the seeded wide-runners in every race, you would usually end up with a few winners: the dogs on the inside struggling for a footing while those that went the long way - the pretty way – ran surefooted round a clear track and finished in front.

At the start all dogs are equal. Each is confined in his own trap but when the electric hare comes by, the lids of the trap fly open. Every dog starts every race from the same point at the same moment. I would be there to enjoy an eight-race card most Fridays, my week's work on local papers at an end. I would drink beer and bet and when Whitefoot Lady or Westpark Bogey came round the outside to finish clear of the rest, the world was indeed a joyful place.

It's easy to debunk this pleasure with reductionist statements and synthetic humour: "What's so fascinating about the fact that one dog can run faster than another?" But the question of which one wins from a plumb-level start is not without its fascination – and besides, what if the one that runs fastest is my dog? Or your dog?

I was brought back to memories of Wimbledon dogs as I reread, not for the first time, *A Question of Upbringing*. The opening chapter can be seen as the pre-race parade: you inspect the runners, you place your bet – it's raining, I'll take the six dog to win, along with a five and six reverse forecast – and then the dogs are loaded into the traps, the hare sets off, no more betting is allowed, and then the traps open and the dogs are racing down the slippery avenues of eternity.

The runners in question in QU are not dogs, nor are they people familiar with dog-racing - but they start level and each once has a race to run. They are of course the four boys leaving school from Le Bas's house: Jenkins, Stringham, Templer and Widmerpool. School ends: the four boys are out on their own, flung into the contemporary world, each with a life to live. So who wins? And who loses?

Well, we must first define our terms. What is success? That, it might be said, is the theme of the entire 12-volume sequence, or one of them. Broadly speaking, we might measure success in three different ways.

1. What we might loosely or traditionally call the father's ambition: that his son makes a mark, does well, is a credit to his family, makes money, becomes a person of substance.

2. The traditional mother's ambition: that her son meets a nice girl, settles down, has children and is happy.

135

3. The personal ambition of each boy: to be the sort of person he chooses to be and to live the sort of life he wants to lead.

Let's look the boys one by one.

Widmerpool

1. It is of course Widmerpool's mother – who had always wanted to be the mother of an MP, her son says – who is full of worldly ambition for her son. And in these terms, Widmerpool is an undoubted success: going great guns at Donners Brebner and then in his own right. He has a good war, or at least is certainly seen as an important figure, and afterwards makes a decent amount of money from business dealings as well as becoming an MP and later a life peer. After that he finds fame as a prominent figure of the counter-culture -- and if things go a bit wonky at the very end, it's doubtful most obituarists would pick up that part of the story.

2. Widmerpool seems never to have an instant of happiness with any of the women he is associated with (except perhaps Pauline the prostitute). He is scorned by Barbara, exploited by Gypsy, rejected brutally by Mildred and taken into a world of horror and betrayal by Pamela. There is scarcely a hint that his emotional *via dolorosa* has had its more enjoyable moments. He has found no comfort, no solace, not an instant of peace.

3. Widmerpool's goal was always worldly success. After his entanglement with Gipsy he vowed never again to allow a woman to interfere with work. To a large extent he achieved this ambition. He also wanted to be admired and respected, and here the results are more equivocal. If he ever does understand the price he paid for his success, and was capable of understanding any questions about it, he would probably tell you that it was well worth it. He sent out to win things: he died as he lived, in the belief that life was a race, and that he was winning. No doubt his old school would be proud of what he achieved: i.e. seizing power. And as usual, the institution would have little or no interest in what he actually did with it.

Templer

1. Templer plays the character of the successful man, and does so convincingly. He starts with money and makes more. He has his problems, like everybody else of his kind, in the slump, but made an impressive recovery and, before the war starts, he is, in Bob Duport's words, doing just about as nicely as you could wish for. He's not ridiculously wealthy, but he's done all right.

2. Templer marries Mona, a trophy wife and the crowning glory of his womanising life. Alas, she is unwilling to play the part required. After she abandons him he picks Betty, another stunner and Mona's opposite in temperament. Her clinging, needy nature, combined with Templer's incurable taste for extra-curricular activities, send her mad. Templer then falls for Pamela, and her rejection drives him to seek his death adventuring in the Balkans. So no: always a short-term success with the ladies: but, either because he's a poor picker or has poor stamina, or both, he is unsuccessful over the long-term.

3. Right from the start it was Templer's ambition is to combine professional success with a damn good time: sympathetic company, plenty to drink, a bit of sport and a lot of women. Here he unquestionably succeeds. "You can't say Peter hasn't been intensive", says Duport. But his ambition fails to change gear. He is unwilling to accept the compromises of marriage that are necessary if you are to enjoy its consolations and rewards. He tries to enjoy maturity with the mind-set

of an adolescent. Had he lived into his 50s he would probably have married a much younger third wife and been an extravagantly devoted father: but – as with some many things in the *Dance* – the war got in the way.

Stringham

1. Stringham gets a great job without troubling to stay at "the" university, and goes to marry an earl's daughter – all this without seeming terribly interested in cither work or marriage. He starts off doing all the right things towards being a great success, but no sooner are the first steps taken than he loses interest. He also loses both job and wife and develops his talent for drinking. He then gets sober – which must have taken a certain amount of ambition – and joins the army with the rank of private. In all obvious respects his career is a disaster.

2. Stringham marries, it seems, despite opposition from both families, but can make nothing of this promising start. He has an affair with Milly Andriadis before his marriage, and walks away from that in a mood of perversity. Perhaps he should have married Tuffy, or run away with Mrs Maclintick – certainly both ladies are very talented at looking-after.

3. What was Stringham's ambition? What and who did he want to be? By what scale should we measure his achievements? Everything he does seems marked by perversity, always presented with impossible urbanity. We see this at Milly's party, at the old boys' dinner, at his mother's party for Moreland's symphony. He seems to be living by a set of rules no one else understands, or has even read, making jokes while doing so. He joins the army from the same mood of perversity: and yet is also surrounded by an air of romantic doom: of complete submission to fate, as he suggested after Temper had crashed his motorcar. He dies, it seems, a good death as a Japanese prisoner of war: still making jokes. Perhaps he fulfilled his ambitions by doing so.

Jenkins

1. Nick is a struggling writer, working first for a publisher, then for a film studio, and after that it's not too clear. He's not making a fortune, and Widmerpool doesn't understand what he's up to. But he's doing OK, he's had a novel published by the first chapter of volume three. In the early part of the war things are going pretty poorly, but they look up later on, when Nick is doing a job he likes and which carries a modest amount of prestige and rank. He's back to the struggling writer stuff in BDFR, working on a book that will never make anyone a fortune, but by TK he's

established as a Writer, with prestige enough to get involved to an international conference. By the last volume he has morphed into a country gent with fancy house and as a writer of sound reputation.

2. In the first three volumes Nick's love life is either futile or dangerously exciting; most of us can relate to that, at least in memory. But by the end of ALM he's ready to marry, and from that moment on, his marriage is presented as cloudlessly happy. He's the only one of the four Etonians to have children.

3. Nick speaks to Widmerpool about his ambitions of becoming a writer when they are both in France in the first volume, though he says he's bluffing at the time. But certainly by the next volume writing is what he wants to do: coming back from Milly Andriadis's party preparing to write a series of essays on life in the style of Montaigne. Soon enough he's a published writer and increasingly a successful one. He is well thought of in artistic circles and, equally important to him, in aristocratic circles. He marries into aristocracy, has children and a nice country house.

Nick's quiet success is important to the structure of Dance. Were he to be a professional failure with a busted marriage Powell would have to write about it, and so Nick would take centre stage and that would spoil the whole thing. If Nick is to be an observer and a chronicler, he has to be in a position to do so: and that's something of a luxury. You've got to be doing all right yourself if you are to spend so much time discussing everybody else. Nick's successful life is a counterpoint to Widmerpool's career, with all its successes and disasters.

Nick's success, and his quiet acceptance of it, might seem a trifle irritating, even a little smug. There's certainly a touch of entitlement there. All the same, his success is essential to the nature of the complete work. The other three characters who left Eton at roughly the same time as Nick all have their chance of a clear run to the winning line -- but like a seeded wide runner at Wimbledon on a rainy Friday night, Nick avoids the trouble, moves surefooted and unimpeded round the outside of the bends and runs on serenely to finish in front, alone.

Magic In Action

Coincidence In *A Dance To The Music Of Time*

*One of the firmest tenets -- so Moreland always said --
in the later teachings of Dr Trelawney was that
coincidence was no more than 'magic in action'.*

Introduction

It will perhaps be a cause of disillusionment
to some readers – to others confirming their worst
suspicions – to learn that the hardest part of writing
novels is not the profoundly moving things the couple
say when at last they confess their love: it's getting
them together in the first place. Never mind the
eternal verities, how do they meet? And often even
more tricky, what brings them together for the second
meet so that things can hot up? The various
scriptwriters of the Fred Astaire film *Top Hat*
contrived a shower of rain in Hyde Park. It forced
Ginger Rogers off her horse to take shelter in a
bandstand. Fred finds the same bandstand and sings:

> *Isn't it a lovely day*
> *To be caught in the rain?*

Which is lovely, but not entirely naturalistic.
So how much does naturalism matter? Many films,
particularly romantic comedies, make something of a
fetish of what is called the Meet Cute. This is a plot-
device, often involving an elaborate coincidence: fate
is forcing the lovers together, almost against their

will. In the film *Notting Hill*, Julia Roberts, as the globally famous film star Anna Scott, walks into the shabby book shop run by Ben Thacker, played by Hugh Grant. She leaves, bedazzling everyone – and then Grant/Thacker goes out for some refreshment, collides with Scott/Roberts in the street and covers her in orange juice. Zing! He offers his adjacent house for a wash and brush-up: on leaving, in a fit of devilment, she kisses him. And we have a story.

This is no more naturalistic than Fred's meet in the bandstand, but it's entirely acceptable in the context of the film and the genre. The audience is easily persuaded to accept the convention of the romantic coincidence, the Meet Cute, and to enjoy this delightful version of reality, just as we accept that when Fred bursts into song an unseen orchestra strikes up. It's not naturalistic but it's great, and we're happy to go along with it. You're not required to believe such coincidences are real: you are politely invited to accept them for the duration of the film, and we do so because they offer a special kind of pleasure: the feeling that life really *should* be like this. We accept the Meet Cute with a full heart, if not a full mind.

We are already in X Trapnel territory here: so we must consider the Heresy of Naturalism. "They think if a writer like me writes the sort of books I do, it's because that's easier, or necessary nowadays. You just look round at what's happening and shove it all down. They can't understand that's not in the least the case. It's just as selective, just as artificial, as if the

144

characters were kings and queens speaking in blank verse."

That's not just true for dialogue; it's also true for plot. The plots in naturalistic novels are also just as selective and artificial as those that involve Shakespearian royalty or Homeric gods. You don't just write down everything that happened to you in the course of a day and call it a novel: *Ulysses*, which at first glance seems precisely that, is just as selective and artificial in its plot as every other novel ever written. And plotting – not the great bravura descriptions or the most luxuriously inventive dialogue – is the hardest part of writing a novel; certainly it's the bit I've always found hardest, though in many ways the most satisfying. Now hear a plain fact: every writer who ever plotted a novel has had to make a decision about coincidence. Or to put that another way: how far can you push your luck? How much will your readers accept? What can you get away with?

In *Brideshead Revisited*, Charles meets Sebastian by a classic if subverted Meet Cute: Sebastian vomits through the open window of Charles's rooms, a clever and rather fancy piece of plotting. Charles first meets Julia, his future love, when she picks him up from the station to visit to her brother Sebastian; this is unflashy, effective, workaday plotting. But the decisive meeting of the novel – in a classic "many years later" trick of the plot – comes when Charles and Julia find themselves by chance on the same transatlantic steamer. Before you can say "that's a bit too convenient" there's a terrible storm and the pair of them, almost the only passengers not seasick, are almost literally thrown together: the only healthy people in a world of the bedridden.

In *Anna Karenina* Anna meets her future lover Vronsky at a railway station. Tolstoy then contrives a ball, where Vronksy chooses to dance with Anna, rather than Kitty, his almost-betrothed, and that changes everything. Anna and Vronsky meet again on a night-train to St Petersburg: the novel is full of trains, but the lives of their passengers keep reaching major junctions and heading off in directions they never – or did they? – intended. Perhaps the process of writing a novel is like advanced physics: every plot is a Hadron Collider in which particles -- characters -- meet by apparent chance to stimulate a colossal release of energy.

Ulysses can seem like a random day in the life of someone not terribly important: Mr Bloom has breakfast, has a bath, goes to a funeral, has a light lunch, and goes about his business of selling advertising space on commission. But as you look more closely you see that this early part of the book is based around the Meet Cute: except that, since this is James Joyce, he had to invent the Unmeet Cute. The two main male characters, Bloom and Stephen, narrowly miss each other in a pair of chance non-meetings, at the newspaper and then at the library, before they meet at last at, of all places, the maternity hospital. By chance. *Ulysses* is a delicate dance of coincidence.

The art of the novel, then, is at least some extent the art of coincidence. In *Goldfinger*, James Bond bumps into someone at an airport, a character who plays an almost infinitely minor role in a previous novel *Casino Royale*. The encounter leads to Bond's first meeting with Goldfinger. And then - as coincidence would have it -- Bond returns to work only to find that his next case involves Goldfinger.

The novel's epigraph is a quotation from its own text: "Goldfinger said, 'Mr Bond, they have a saying in Chicago: once is happenstance, twice is coincidence, the third time it's enemy action.'" The novel is in three parts: Happenstance, Coincidence, and Enemy Action. It's the best contents page in the history of thrillers.

In my first novel *Rogue Lion Safaris* I introduced a large and frightening animal – it turns out to be a giraffe -- to throw the couple together at the crucial moment; plausible enough, since the story is set in the African bush. Powell brings Jenkins together with Jean after a chance meeting with her brother in the Ritz and the stimulus of "an electrically illuminated young lady in a bathing costume", more plausible than you might think since the figure – the installation – was once a genuine feature of the Great West Road.

Novelists walk a tightrope of plausibility. They must bring their characters together for scenes of love and hate without causing the reader to suspend disbelief. The longer the novel, the more fraught that danger is. Comparisons with Powell and Proust are, I suppose inevitable: and Proust is also keen on coincidence. In the third volume *A l'ombre de jeunes filles en fleur*, the painter Elstir coincidentally knows the seaside girls who have excited the Narrator's interest; the Narrator's grandmother coincidentally meets her old and well-connected friend Madame de Villeparisis at Balbec; coincidentally the lustful Baron de Charles takes a fancy to the Narrator at the same resort. It may not be entirely plausible – or to put that another way, it may not be entirely naturalistic – but the enraptured and accepting reader is carried along by the power of the novel.

For Powell the problem is a great deal more acute. *A la recherhe du temps perdu* is largely about the inner life of the Narrator, and his curious relationship with external activities. *Dance* is a novel about human interactions, in which the first person narrator is for the most past observer and recorder, rather than philosophising participant. A novel structured on that basis is going to require a lot of meetings, and that means a lot coincidences. The novelist can do everything possible to makes these meetings seamless and inevitable and totally unremarkable, so that you hardly even notice them, which is a hard task over a dozen volumes: or he/she can go the other way and make a big thing of them. If the novelist is Anthony Powell he can turn a potential weakness of the structure into the king-pole, the very thing that gives the 12-volume novel its strength and power and durability. In a sense Powell does both at once: but it is the second kind of coincidence that wins.

To try and understand what he does, we can take a look at the 11 Modesty Blaise novels by Peter O'Donnell. These are marvellous thrillers, full of fantasy and imagination, plotted with taut brilliance. After the second novel it has become clear that the would-be ruthless head of the British Secret Service, Sir Gerald Tarrant, is far too smitten with Modesty to send her off on any more lethal assignments.

Partly from consistency of character, but I suspect mostly from delight in his virtuoso plotting skills, O'Donnell launches Modesty into nine subsequent novel-length adventures by coming up with nine epic coincidences: she is present at an assassination attempt, she makes an emergency landing in her Cessna and finds two bad men beating up a doctor; she rescues a man while making a solo crossing of the Tasman Sea; the bad men try and kidnap her companion on a canoe-trip through the wilderness.

These coincidences set the tone: Modesty is "incurably trouble-prone": and just as well, too, or the bad men would win every time. The coincidences set Modesty aside as someone very special: singled out by fate to take part in these uplifting adventures: an angel sent by the power of coincidence to set things aright. Thus a potential weakness – getting Modesty into trouble again – is turned into a position of strength.

Powell pulls off a similar trick. He takes the potential weakness of his chosen form – what ho, Stringham, golly-gosh, not Widmerpool again – and

149

makes it the power, strength and meaning of the entire enterprise.

In other words, improbability itself can be turned into an asset for the novelist. In *The Hitchhiker's Guide to the Galaxy* Douglas Adams writes "If you hold a lungful of air you can survive in the total vacuum of space for about 30 seconds. However... what with space being the mind-boggling size it is, the chances of getting picked up by another ship within those thirty seconds are two to the power of two hundred and seventy six thousand, seven hundred and nine to one against. By a totally staggering coincidence that is also the telephone number of an Islington flat where Arthur once went to a very good party and met a very nice girl whom he totally failed to get off with."

Arthur and his companion, breath-holding in the vastness of space, after being evicted from the ship they had hitched a ride on, do indeed find another. It is called the Heart of Gold and it's powered by a revolutionary device called the Infinite Improbability Drive: one that makes the most far-fetched coincidence inevitable.

By coincidence, the idea of the inevitable coincidence is discussed in the Modesty Blaise novel *The Silver Mistress*. The name of the Macanese banker Wu Smith comes up twice in quick succession in different contexts. Modesty's sidekick Willie Garvin explains: "It's the flux."

Modesty elaborates: "Willie calls it the flux...
he doesn't believe that coincidences are coincidences.
He says there's a magnetic flux about the earth which
causes like events to occur simultaneously or in
sequence. Open *The Times Literary Supplement* and
you find three different people have written books
about Queen Victoria's third cousin twice removed
who was Governor of the Honduras or something. All
published in the same month. And nobody ever heard
of him before. It's the flux."

Coincidence has been savoured and studied in
the search for deeper spiritual and scientific
understanding of the way life works. In 1952 Carl
Jung published a paper *Synchronicity: an Acausal
Connecting Principle*. His idea was that synchronous
events and apparent coincidences are manifestations
of our spiritual lives, and represent the underlying
order that governs them. In this he had support from
two Nobel laureates, Albert Einstein and Wolfgang E
Pauli (of the Exclusion Principle). Einstein remarked:
"Coincidence is God's way of remaining
anonymous." It is also the novelist's way of keeping
God out of the text: coincidence *ex machina* is the
way that naturalistic novels tend to work.

Einstein and Pauli were interested in the
interconnectedness of all the elementary particles in
the universe: and if you grasp even something of what
that implies, you're likely to agree that bumping into
your oldest friend in an Army mess no longer looks
like the most impossible thing in creation.

The entomologist Philip Howse wrote, in his study of the death's head hawk moth *The Bee Tiger*: "Synchronicity challenges our firmly engrained concepts of the universe and the nature of human existence. It is not accessible to statistical evaluation and scientific study." It implies an order behind the chaos... and that is a subject that scientists and philosophers can argue about throughout eternity. However, another plain fact: making apparent order from chaos is at the heart of the novelist's job. That, in short, is what a story means: a story makes a pattern that humans respond to. Perhaps Dr Trelawney was trying to do the same thing in the course of his career in magic as documented in the *Dance*.

So let us look further into the question of coincidence, magic and improbability. I invite you to stroll with me through the 12 volumes of the *Dance*, taking a look at each coincidence as it comes and trying to work out if the build-up of coincidence has a cumulative effect. I propose to give each coincidence a plausibility rating, from the one-star coincidence of meeting Moreland in a pub, to five-star coincidences that test the both writer and reader to the maximum. The following list is not exhaustive, but I think I've covered all the major ones.

It is also my suspicion that each novel has a single central coincidence from which most of the action and most of the meaning of the volume depend: coincidence as fulcrum. Those that seem to have such significance I will mark with a dagger†, as if they were wicket-keepers.

A Question of Upbringing

The scope for coincidence increases exponentially with the length of the narrative. It follows that the first volume has fewer and less dramatic coincidences than the last: the effect is by its nature cumulative. By the last volume the coincidences are travelling in packs. At the same time, it's important for Powell to establish coincidence as his working method right from the start: to make it clear that coincidence is not just a plotting device: to let the reader know that coincidence is the book's meaning as well as its method. This is both an essential courtesy and a way of establishing the essential rhythm of the work: coincidences that come not as a series of shocks but as part of the inevitable pattern of the narrative. In this way the novelist seeks to create order from the chaos of existence.

So after the enigmatic opening passage around the brazier, a humdrum street scene fraught with hints of eternal significance, we move into the narrative proper and are introduced to the concept of coincidence by way of a chance encounter with Widmerpool. "This vision of Widmerpool", as Powell describes it, completing his solitary run, training for a team for which he will never be selected, is not just the first appearance of Widmerpool but also the first chance meeting, the first appearance of coincidence... though it's not exactly a coincidence, it can't be, since we as readers have met neither character before – but it's clearly a highly charged event. Even so, Powell, with his love of understatement, half throws it away.

153

Readers who fail to pick it up will do so retrospectively, as the narrative marshes on.

**Arrival of Uncle Giles

The first chapter turns around the unexpected arrival of Uncle Giles at Nick's school: a chance event that throws the routines of school life into disorder. As a direct result, Stringham and Templer both find themselves at odds with their house-master, Le Bas.

*Meeting with Le Bas in the field

This chance meeting, not at all implausible, leads to the Braddock alias Thorne incident, showing both Le Bas's ineffectiveness and Stringham's mastery – and also his recklessness. It's clear that there is something dangerous about Stringham, for there is more than japery in this jape.

**Widmerpool witnesses Le Bas's arrest

That Widmerpool, described in such profusion of detail in the opening pages, should be there at the vital moment is a useful coincidence in terms of plot-making. Widmerpool discusses the event in terms of shock and horror: no hint of schoolboy delight or mischief-making, and this confirms his already-established oddness. Stringham mocks him to his face, but so cleverly that Widmerpool hardly notices.

The second chapter, as Jenkins visits the homes of Stringham and Templer, is without coincidence – save the teasing line at the end, when Jenkins and Sunny Farebrother part and Farebrother "passed out of my life for some twenty years". That is a quiet way of telling the reader that there is a great deal more of this sort of stuff to come. A tone has been set.

† ****Widmerpool at La Grenadiere

This is the central coincidence of the first volume: after an elaborate introduction to the place and its personnel, Jenkins finds himself "face to face with Widmerpool". It is clear in this instant that both coincidence and Widmerpool are of central importance to the entire work. It is like a slap in the face: wise up! This is how the book works, and pay attention, because Widmerpool, already scorned as the boy who didn't matter, matters. And so he does: as the chapter continues with Widmerpool's actions in the dispute between Monsieur Örn and Monsieur Lundquist, Powell drops another marvellously teasing hint of what will follow: "Even then I did not recognise the quest for power."

*Templer calls in at "the" university

It is not exactly a coincidence that Stringham and Jenkins both go to "the" university, there being, of course, only one; it's only a mild coincidence that Templer should pay a visit, and that he should bring a pair of his own friends to create a notably disharmonious party. But the pattern of bringing together people fundamentally out of sympathy with each other has been established: after the awkwardness of Sillery's tea-party comes the still greater awkwardness of this visit, one that ends forever the friendship between Temper and Stringham.

*Le Bas at Oxford

Another one-star coincidence, and one without any vast plot-points: but it continues the pattern of recurrent meetings and keeps Le Bas in play.

Stringham swerves a dinner-date

This is not exactly a coincidence: it is in fact a non-coincidence: a meeting that did not take. But it needs to be noted: the chance invitation from Lady Bridgnorth "effortlessly snapped one of the links... between Stringham and myself". This is coincidence as a sundering, a chance parting rather than chance meeting: and yet it changes Nick's life.

A Buyer's Market

This volume begins with an elaborate set-up, which prepares the way for book's central coincidence – or coincidences, for BM turns on a pair of them. These introductory pages contain two successive flashbacks before the narrative proper starts; each of these contains a significant chance meeting. The first is with Mr Deacon at the Louvre, the second is with Barbara in Hyde Park. "This was to be the last day for many months that I woke up in the morning without immediately thinking of Barbara."

The book starts with the sale of Mr Deacon's paintings somewhere in the unspecified future, moving on to memories of Mr Deacon from Nick's childhood, and then, having flashed both forward and back, and taken in the pleasant recollections of Hyde Park, we are back the chronological narrative, with Nick superstitiously gazing at a painting by Mr Deacon at the house where he is to dine that night and, he hopes, enjoy the company of Barbara and later dance with her.

**Widmerpool at the Walpole-Wilsons

Widmerpool's arrival at the same dinner takes Nick aback. At this point there is a brief aside: "I did not however as yet see him as one of those symbolic figures, of whom most people possess at least one example, round whom the past and the future have a way of assembling." This is a brief summary of the operating principle of the *Dance*, and it can be compared with Willie Garvin's theory of "the flux" in the Modesty Blaise novels. Widmerpool is as hard to assimilate at the dinner as he was at school or at La Grenadière. But we learn that he considers himself the backbone of the system of debs' dances, a standard spare man. His passion for Barbara is revealed, along with its dramatic rejection, in a manner that is comic, painful and cruel.

Later in the book Nick reflects on the way that he had fallen in with Widmerpool, and the way that evening had panned out, musing on "the extraordinary process that causes certain figures to appear and reappear in the performance of one or another sequence of a ritual dance". This is rare example of Powell putting his cards on the table: demanding that we accept his premise that, for reasons beyond easy explanation, the same people occur and reoccur in the course of a lifetime. In JM Barrie's *Peter Pan*, the audience is invited to "clap if you believe in fairies". Powell is making a similar invitation here: read on -- but only if you are prepared to accept the inevitable nature of coincidence. His defence of this proposition would not be entirely convincing if this was an essay on life (in the manner of Montaigne, perhaps), but as a literary convention, as an exhortation to suspend disbelief, as a demand to accept that there is something ever-so-slightly magical about ordinary life, it is compelling. And it is Widmerpool's appearance, more than anything else, that makes it so.

†***Meeting Mr Deacon

This is not entirely a narrative coincidence because we haven't met Mr Deacon in the course of the book's chronological narrative. But it's a chance meeting and a very important one, one that will allow Nick to become part of a raffish artistic set, a liberating change from the unexciting companions of the evening till that point.

†**Meeting Stringham

These twin coincidences -- the meetings in Grosvenor Place and Hyde Park Corner, five minutes apart, take this ad-hoc group to Milly Andriadis's party in Hill Street, ten minutes further on, where a new kind of world is opened up to Jenkins: worldly, power-conscious and with a different set of rules. Here Widmerpool begins his intimacy with Gipsy Jones and is introduced by her to left-wing opinion; it is one of the turning-points of his life.

**Sillery at Mrs Andriadis's party

Sillery acts as a kind of guide, like Virgil to Dante, explaining to Nick the way this new world operates: how power functions in this fascinating and troubling environment.

***Uncle Giles in Shepherd Market

The mysterious appearance of Uncle Giles brings to an end this long and winding evening. It is a pleasingly banal moment -- "I've been having trouble with my teeth" -- after an evening of complex and exhilarating discoveries, and one that makes no direct contribution to plot. It's a coming down to earth: an acceptance that this was not in fact the moment to compose a series of essays on human life and character in the manner of Montaigne. It's a hot evening, a point that's been made several times: why, then, is Uncle Giles wearing a "discreetly horsey overcoat with the collar turned up"?

***Jean at Stourwater

Nick is taken to on a visit to Sir Magnus Donners at Stourwater. He finds himself sitting next to Jean Templer at lunch, and a spark is struck between them as they discuss the tapestry depicting the sin of

159

lust. At least it's a step-on from Nick's ineffectiveness at the Templer house; and it leaves a hint that there is more to come, for by this stage the reader is getting used to the long wavelengths of plotting that are required in this extended form of narrative.

*Gypsy arrives at Mr Deacon's shop

Gypsy turns up on the day of Mr Deacon's funeral – "that was a desperate affair" – which she refused to attend. Nick has been left alone by Mr Deacon's lodger Barnby, who has been summoned by Baby Wentworth. Gipsy decides to make a surprise by dressing up in her Eve costume. She and Nick make something approximating to love among the antique shawls.

And this is perhaps the real coincidence of this volume: not a coincidence of action, but the coincidence that both Nick and Widmerpool find themselves involved with the same woman not once but twice. In a sense Nick can be said to have come off better: he frees himself from Barbara without the public humiliation that Widmerpool undergoes, and he succeeds in having his way with Gypsy without any emotional or financial involvement; Widmerpool, fairly deeply involved on both these counts, fails to win any physical favours from Gypsy himself.

But this assessment is examined much later in TKO, four volumes later, when Nick and Moreland discuss the question of living intensely over late night bacon and eggs in the Hay Loft. Moreland asks: "Is it better to love someone and not have them. Or have

160

somebody and not love them? I mean from the point of view of action – living intensely. Does action consist in having or loving?"

This is a fairly exact description of Widmerpool's and Nick's experiences with Gypsy. Nick had (I think we can assume) merely lost his virginity, a step that allows him to move on. Widmerpool has found a new way of looking at the world.

The Acceptance World

The third volume of the *Dance* is unique in that Nick's own actions and feelings take centre stage. For this volume only he's not just an observer, he's also the major participant. AW is about Nick's love affair with Jean; my father, a romantic to the end, saw the thread of Nick's still-persisting love for Jean extending through every subsequent volume.

Naturally this affair is also a lens through which Nick/Powell observes the doings of other characters involved in the pursuit and capture of love: coincidences that make love seem all the more baffling: Stripling with Mrs Erdleigh and Jean; Mrs Erdleigh with Uncle Giles and Stripling; Mona with Templer and Quiggin; Anne Stepney with Barnby and Dicky Umfraville; Jean with Stripling and Duport as well as Nick.

But Jean and Nick are at the heart of it all. The volume is heavy with nostalgia for lost days of passion, the sort of passion that makes everything else in life utterly trivial and most days either miserable or ecstatic – or both in rapid succession, as we see at the end. AW is also full of sharp memories of what happens when things go wrong in love: when the balance of power is disastrously disturbed.

The first chapter takes in tea at the Ufford with Uncle Giles, and a chance meeting with Mrs Erdleigh, which sets up the subsequent coincidental meeting.

The book contains two multiple chance meetings, both involving five people. In each one, every person among the the five either loses or gains a partner, sometimes both. The first of these occurs across a succession of three chance meetings at the Ritz.

***Nick meets Templer

Nick, waiting for Mark Members in these lush surroundings, bumps into Templer, on top of his form, cheerful, witty, hospitable. He's the perfect antidote to Nick's mounting irritation about the no-showing Members: suddenly all is convivial. Perhaps Members chose the Ritz to put Nick at a disadvantage: by the end of it, Nick is not complaining.

**Quiggin arrives

This is unexpected, but all is explained when we learn that Quiggin has taken over Members's job, and is now acting for the novelist St John Clarke.

162

†*Jean arrives with Mona

Since Templer is there, it is no great stretch to bring in his wife and his sister. A slow-burn attraction between Jean and Nick is established from the start – and also, though we don't grasp this until later, between Mona and Quiggin. In the aftermath of this five-way meeting, Templer ends up wifeless, Mona links up Quiggin and Jean and Nick embark on a thrilling, tender and above all secret love affair.

***Members in the Park: the political demonstration

Nick runs into Members in Hyde Park between the Isbister Memorial Exhibition (where he has bumped into a number of characters, including Sillery) and Jean's borrowed flat in Rutland Gate. They discuss the ousting of Members from the Clarke household and Quiggin's infiltration. Together they watch a group marching in a political cause, in which St John Clarke is propelled in a wheelchair by Quiggin and Mona. Nick proceeds to Jean's place, where she opens the door to him naked.

The second meeting of five takes place at Foppa's club. Jean and Nick deicide to go there after a bout of love followed by a row caused by the – to Nick –horrifying discovery that Jean has had an affair with Jimmy stripling.

*Barnby and Anne Stepney at Foppa's

163

The club, a favourite spot for both Nick and Barnby, brings them together with each other's partners.

***Dicky Umfraville at Foppa's

Umfraville rises from his game of cards with Foppa and introduces himself. We have heard of Umfraville before from Sillery and Stringham, but not met him. He is at once overwhelming: charming: funny: reckless: a perfect antidote to oppressive politics and the intermittences of love. All four seem delighted to fall in with him. What he says of Foppa holds good for himself: "No nonsense about economics or world disarmament with him."

By the end of the novel Umfraville and Anne are married, Jean is on the way to a return to her husband, and Nick and Barnby are about to find themselves abandoned and alone.

At Lady Molly's

So far as I was concerned, this was the volume that changed everything. At single stroke, a single *coup de roman*, I understood, in the manner of a Zen student finding enlightenment, what the whole 12-volume sequence was about, how it worked, the time-scale on which it was constructed and why I had to go on reading it. I had read the first three volumes as and when, over the course of about a year; I read the rest in about three months and then started all over again.

164

ALM begins with recollections of a childhood visit to the Conyers's flat and the arrival of the infinitely dashing Mildred Blaides. We then shift back to the default time of the narrative, by now 1934, and Chips Lovell's suggestion to Nick that they pay a visit to Lady Molly.

**Mrs Conyers at Molly's
In this chance meeting we learn that Mrs Conyers sister, Mildred was about to arrive with her new fiancé.

†††**** Arrival of Mildred with Widmerpool as her fiancé

Here is coincidence in the form of masterpiece: I give it three daggers because it is the pivotal coincidence of the entire sequence. Widmerpool had not even been mentioned in the volume at that point, so Powell was taking a hell of a gamble. True, there's a new-reader's catch-up offered a little later, but this is a coincidence that comes without warning... and those readers who have been with Powell all along are massively rewarded with this sudden a revelation of a quasi-magical incident. It is clear at once that the seizing and the abandonment of partners is essential to the great dance that we have been invited to watch, or if you prefer, have no alternative but to take part in.

"Life is full of internal dramas, instantaneous and sensational, played out to an audience of one." Here is the sentence that, perhaps above all others in the *Dance* that has stayed with me. This arrival of Widmerpool and Mildred is the perfect revelation of the principle of coincidence as magic in action. No one can grasp its significance but Nick – and every reader of the *Dance*.

From this moment it's clear that Widmerpool is not just an important character like Stringham or Templer. He is now unmistakably central to the entire project, to the way the plot has already unfolded and will continue to unfold. Nick and Widmerpool are in this together until the end. How and why this is the case will be revealed by looking back at what is already past - and by reading on.

And then we are back in the rhythm of the *Dance* once again, and in a gentler fashion, we follow the course of coincidence in the now accustomed manner.

*Meeting Frederica and Norah

Nick meets Frederica at the Conyers flat, and they drop in at the flat shared by Norah and Eleanor.

**Meeting Quiggin in cinema queue

A chance meeting that leads to an invitation to visit Quiggin and Mona in the country – one that leads eventually to Nick's invitation to Thrubworth.

†*Meeting Isobel at Thrubworth

166

Nick meets Isobel, who is visiting her brother and knows at once that he will marry her. This meeting is pivotal to the structure of this volume; the earlier meeting with Widmerpool is pivotal to the entire sequence.

*Meeting Tuffy at Molly's

An accustomed to place to find Tuffy; she gives news of Stringham and his drinking.

*** Jeavons at the pub.

Jeavons is after drink, Nick food, but both are prepared to seek adventure. Jeavons suggests they try Dicky Umfraville's night club.

*** Arrival of Templer, Widmerpool, Mildred Haycock and Mrs Taylor or Porter at the night-club

Here is Powell on top form, hurling characters together and seeing what will happen. Jeavons explains his wartime dalliance with Mildred to Nick, doubling the coincidental value of this meeting, and later reminds Mildred, who had quite forgotten. Widmerpool leaves, very poorly, to Mildred's complete unconcern.

*** General Conyers's story

It takes a little – but not too much -- forcing of the pace to set up General Conyers as the narrator of Widmerpool's downfall by way of his failure in bed with Mildred. Perhaps it's more an example of adroit plotting rather than magic in action: but Conyers, neither gloating nor heavily humorous, tells the tale well, and with an almost Powellian detachment.

And it's at this point we are aware of the hidden coincidence that has guided the narrative of this volume: the fact that Nick and Widmerpool are yet again linked in love. This time round, both become engaged and both to the daughter of an earl, though different daughters and different earls. One engagement ends in disaster, the other continues in the best possible manner.

Casanova's Chinese Restaurant

The volume begins with a flash-forward to post-war years and the contemplation of a bombed pub; this is at once followed by a flashback to the period at the end of BM, three volumes back, though at the same time we are aware that the default timeline is now at 1933. It's all accomplished with enviable neatness. The flashback from post-war to 1928/9 is occasioned by a coincidence, one that has something almost knowingly mystical about it: the appearance of the itinerant prima donna of the highways singing *Kashmiri Love Song*. This sequence introduces us to Moreland, whisking us back to the late 20s and the pages at once dance to his wit and charm, his edgy nature, and the affection that Nick has for him right from the start, which is made obvious by the opening flash-forward.

*Meeting with Mr Deacon

Nick enters the Mortimer to meet Barnby, and finds Mr Deacon, whom he now sees regularly. He is introduced to Moreland, Maclintick, Gossage and Carolo: at once plunging us all into Bohemian life, pubs, restaurants, art, friendships, gossip and the start of Nick's intimacy with Moreland.

*Dinner at Casanova's

Against hardly a coincidence: a chance mixing of art-minded people and some excellent conversation: painter, writer, musician, music critic.

**Mrs Foxe at the theatre

A minor coincidence, save for the fact that the nature of the *Dance* is that Nick can hardly cross the road without bumping into someone he knows, for good or ill. Here the world of "a shabby lot of highbrows" (words of Mark Members) makes a tentative coming-together with that of Society.

***Mrs Foxe and Chandler

The greater coincidence is that Mrs Foxe has fallen for Chandler in a big way: Society approaching Bohemia as a suitor, offering all sorts of inducements, including "a rather ritzy life". And everybody likes being fallen in love with. Mrs Foxe, out of place among the highbrows, is nonetheless determined to sweep Chandler into her orbit.

***St John Clarke at Hyde Park Gardens

169

After the first chapter's excursion into Bohemian life we are at a rather stuffy lunch party, with a great gathering of Nick's aristocratic in-laws. Clarke, representing (Nick's view) arts and letters in a somewhat debased form, has invited himself because of his friendship with Erridge (another brother-in-law, now in Spain), one inspired, it seems, by their shared political disillusionment. Here is St John Clarke, out of place in this sort of aristocratic family gathering, but determined to get what he needs from it.

**Nursing home: Moreland

Many of the Powellian coincidences are made acceptable in terms of the naturalistic conventions on which the narrative is based: Nick inhabits a small world or perhaps two small worlds: These are based in two small parts of London: Society and the upper classes in Belgravia, the Bohemian world in Fitzrovia. So far so straightforward. But it's a slightly odd that Matilda should be in the same smart nursing-home as Isobel.

***Nursing home: Widmerpool

Once again, the art and the non-art worlds collide as Widmerpool is discovered at the same nursing-home: Widmerpool and Moreland at once quite out of sympathy.

†*Mrs Foxe's party: arrival of Stringham

Mrs Foxe is persuaded by Chandler to give a party for Moreland's symphony. This generous act sets up a collision between two worlds, a mixture of guests that would grace any drawing-rooms in Society coming up against the saloon bar of the Mortimer. Nick is an exception, an amphibian, equally at home in both words, not fully committed to either.

These unlike elements are brought to the point of explosion with the arrival of Stringham, drunk in a manner familiar to those who have overdone the tequila: the certainty that you're not drunk, just overwhelmingly wonderful. He is perfectly at ease, captivating both Moreland and Mrs Maclinktick as he holds forth on the perils of marriage. This glorious set-piece has added force because Moreland, empathically of Bohemia, and Priscilla, an aristocrat's daughter, are in the process of falling in love as this scene plays out all around them. This four-handed encounter across the novel's great cultural divide is packed with mutual incomprehensibilities – so it is perhaps inevitable that a quatrefoil cup perused by Lord Huntercombe turned out to be a forgery.

The book reaches its conclusion with Maclintick's descent into despair: the awful visit to his home after his wife has left, and his subsequent suicide. There is no further play of coincidence in the volume, save an important negative coincidence: as Moreland points out, Maclintick very considerately refrains from killing himself on the evening that Moreland and Nick visit him. There is an awful decency, and a generosity to his greatest friend, in that decision to hold off for another day or two. It's also good literary manners: a characteristic Powellian avoidance of melodrama: no sequence in which Nick and Moreland enter the gas-filled house to find the body.

The Kindly Ones

There are five, maybe six coincidences of four-star level and above in this volume, but it is dominated by a pair of one-star coincidences that make clear the shatteringly personal impact of historical events: in both cases, the coming of war. This is not war with all its historical and global implications, this is war as something almost domestic, war as something that will and must change individuals as well as nations, altering their lives irrevocably while making them even more like themselves.

*Dr Trelawney and General Conyers at Stonehurst

The two exchange greetings as Trelawney passes with his disciples, showing again the General's breadth of interests.

*Arrival of Uncle Giles at Stonehurst.

There is nothing remarkable – only exasperating, at least to Nick's father – about Uncle Giles's paying a visit to his brother. But he comes bearing the news of the assassination of Archduke Franz Ferdinand: an event which must, as General Conyers at once understands, lead swiftly to war. This self-obsessed, faintly ludicrous figure announces a cataclysm that will destroy millions.

****Templer at Stourwater

The fact that the Morelands and the Jenkinses are to spend an evening at Stourwater, home of "the great industrialist" Sir Magnus Donners, is another collision between two worlds, of the kind that dominated the previous volume; and there are hints that Matilda - who reached the world of Society and power through her earlier association with Donners, only to hook up with Moreland and align herself with Bohemia - is thinking of making a return.

The division between the two worlds is made clear by the chance arrival of Peter Templer, Nick's old school friend, as fellow-guest of Sir Magnus Donners: rackety, quite indifferent to the arts, feeling only a breezy contempt for the unconventionally dressed Morelands. The evening turns out to be more like Bohemia than Society: and Templer, warming up, finds some escape from the troubles of his own life by behaving in a fashion more Bohemian than the Bohemians.

***   Anne Umfraville at Stourwater

Anne is a Society person who has been trying to live as a Bohemian, associated for a while with Barnby. It's surprising first to find her involved with Donners, and then flattered by Temper's attentions. Donners makes Matilda play the part of the Envy in the masque of the Seven Deadly Sins: if indeed she envied Anne's position she didn't waste much time about taking it over.

†*   Arrival of Widmerpool

Hardly surprising that Widmerpool should pay a late-night call on Donners, for the two are working very closely, But it's startling that he appears in uniform: "Nothing, up to that date, had so much brought home to me the imminence, the certitude of war," Nick comments. This pairing of Uncle Giles and Widmerpool as the unlikely heralds of global war is itself a beautifully managed coincidence. The appearance of Uncle Giles with such momentous news in the first chapter is sinister, alarming and slightly ludicrous: so is this appearance of Widmerpool with his battledress and his swagger stick. But this time things are still more terrible, partly because of what we already know about Widmerpool, and partly because this second announcement of war must have a much greater effect on Nick the narrator and on the story he is narrating.

****Duport at the Bellevue
****Dr Trelawney at the Bellevue
***Mrs Erdleigh at the Bellevue

We have been introduced to the idea of magic and the paranormal in the first chapter, with the Stourwater ghost and Trelawney's cult. It is notable that Nick/Powell never expresses the slightest cynicism about the ghost: there is no easy credulousness, but no come-off-it denial either.

Ghosts are accepted, in maturity and in childhood, as an aspect of everyday life "almost an amenity".

It follows that when Albert, servant at Stonehurst, turns up again as proprietor of the Bellevue, there is a faint whiff of magical possibilities: at once manifest in the appearance of Duport, Temper's crony and Jean's husband, hiding from his creditors. This might have stretched credibility in earlier volumes, but we have been softened up. We are now always on our toes, expecting coincidence: we have learned that it is part of the stock-in-trade of the *Dance*, part of its force. With the many hints of magic in this chapter we begin to accept that the narrative method of the *Dance* is not entirely naturalistic. We have already been schooled to accept the somewhat improbable as perfectly normal: at this point there is a distinct escalation. Duport, Dr Trelawney, Mrs Erdleigh: such a triple coming-together would have been unacceptable in volume one, but now we are prepared to go along with it.

It wouldn't do to overstate this, but there is the smallest prevision of magical realism in the pattern of coincidences in this chapter, and by extension, in the entire sequence of 12 volumes. Duport's arrival is thrilling and beguiling, and will surely reveal some secrets about what and who unites the two men: for after all, they have both loved and both been loved by the same woman – and, as more is revealed, both have been made fools of by her. Duport already knows this: Nick is forced to accept it.

The magical theme continues with the rescue of Dr Trelawney from the bathroom and his subsequent high-flown rhetoric about love and war. This scene brought to an end by the infinitely soothing presence of Mrs Erdleigh, high priestess with a syringe. Perhaps it was her presence there that drew both Uncle Giles and Dr Trelawney to the seaside town: either way she turns up to the funeral – the only mourner besides Nick – dressed in widow's weeds, later to be the sole beneficiary of his will. Trelawney is, as he was in the first chapter, a plausible sham: we are invited to believe in Mrs Erdleigh, at least to an extent.

***General Conyers's fiancée

She turns out to be Mrs Weedon or Tuffy, last seen recapturing Stringham, now effortlessly capturing this more formidable but less elusive person. The General's enthusiasm for life and his basic toughness is shown by his taking on so formidable a partner; we are also once again aware of Tuffy's talent for looking-after: "her taste, in short, for power"

***Widmerpool wants to visit Molly

The fact that Widmerpool's mother is involved with Molly Jeavons in her attempt to dodge evacuees is just about acceptable; after all, Molly is always arranging things with the most unlikely people. Powell continues to play a kind of grandmother's footsteps game with plausibility. This coincidence is principally a plot-device, one that allows Widmerpool and Nick to set off together in the direction of Molly's home.

****Gypsy Jones addressing the crowd

This is another rather startling coincidence: not least because we have learned from Quiggin that Gypsy is "well looked on by the party", so would presumably be above such chores as haranguing passers-by. Maybe she likes to go out into the streets every now and then to keep in touch with the People. Nick is startled by Widmerpool's horror, his terror that she might recognise him and speak to him. Is Widmerpool dismayed because he is now emphatically on the opposite side to her? Or is it because she knows of his commitment to the left? We have already been told that he is "far from a Tory" and that his views have moved "steadily to the left". But – on a purely nosy professional level – I would love to know whether Powell was already planning to involve Widmerpool, as a possible crypto-communist, in an espionage scandal, and as a presumed traitor, in a later volume.

****Moreland at Lady Molly's

The war has already begun to disrupt lives and tear people apart, no matter how far they are from the front line. Moreland's unlikely appearance at Molly's house confirms the fact that life is already utterly out of joint. Moreland, abandoned by Matilda and forced even to abandon his cat, his one remaining comforter, is barely managing to cope. War has almost undone him already, even though hostilities have hardly started. It's possible that Moreland might have put that another way.

*Quiggin, Members and Anne Umfraville at the Scarlet Pimpernel

An uncomfortable meeting; different people preparing for total war in their different ways. Anne has returned to Bohemia; Quiggin it seems, has a taste for Templer's exes.

****Jeavons's brother Stanley

No shock that Stanley should visit his brother's house, from which none are turned away: but this amiable, humdrum meeting allows Nick to get his commission and join the army, something neither his father, General Conyers nor Widmerpool could bring about.

This is a volume as richly stuffed with coincidences as Christmas cake is stuffed with fruit. The pace and probability of the coincidences are both hotting up, more is being asked of us as the sequence continues, but we hardly notice. That's because the book is dominated by the terrible coincidence of one World War following another after an interlude of just 21 years. And Nick must now submit to it. The sword of Mithras flashes from its scabbard, as Dr Trelawney said: and if this is magic in action, it is of a truly terrible kind.

The Valley of Bones

So, here's a bold step for a roman fleuve: just past the halfway point you set your entire and by-now familiar cast to one side and introduce a load of characters never met before, making complete break in continuity. This is certainly faithful to Nick's (and/ or Powell's) experience, but it's a big ask of the reader. We must now be as entranced by Gwatkin, Kedward, Bithel and Sayce as we have been by Widmerpool, Stringham and Templer and the other Etonians.

Presumably those who write Powell off as a snob never got so far as this (or beyond the first chapter of the first volume). Certainly this is a strong counter-argument to that notorious claim: Powell uses the same tone -- educated, ironic, dispassionate, generous, occasionally affectionate, sometimes cynical, mostly unjudging -- for Gwatkin as for the Earl of Warminster. They are equally ludicrous, equally valid, equally significant, equally dignified, equally valid human beings. This drastic shift of cast and narrative is a hard trick to pull off, but I'd say Powell carries the day largely because of Bithel.

Not only have we a bunch of new characters, we are also deprived of coincidence, for who can Nick encounter by chance in Wales and Northern Ireland? The first half of the book strips Powell down to the bones as a novelist (perhaps a reason for the title). He is without familiar characters and without his most familiar device, no old pals turning up every time a door opens -- and yet he still has us turning the

179

pages, wondering what Bithel will do next and what will become of poor Gwatkin.

At last in the third chapter Jenkins gets away, first on a course and then on leave. He is back in England, among his own, and Powell takes the opportunity to chuck a pile of coincidences at us in his most lavish fashion: as if his readers were as nostalgic for coincidence as Nick is for family and familiarity. The final scene at Frederica's house has the brilliant plotting of a Feydeau farce. We readers are so happy to be among familiar people again (just as Nick is) that we're not too worried by plausibility. It's just good to be home: or as near as what counts for home in wartime: and at home in the land of coincidence.

*Pennistone on the train

It's always good to meet a sympathetic person in unsympathetic circumstances, and the faint connection -- they were both at Milly Andriadis's party – is also nice.

*Barnby in London

Here Nick and Barnby, two fellow-artists meet and discuss what they are doing in wartime. Barnby is using his talents; Nick, clearly, is not. Shortly we shall learn from Nick that at Castlemallock "I knew despair".

**Brent on the course

180

Not too surprising to re-meet a person met only once, though only Nick knows how much they have in common: for Brent too has been among Jean's lovers. As ever, Nick delights both in his own secretiveness and the soul-baring of others. Almost no one but Jean herself knows about her affair with Nick, though later we learn that Isobel has probably guessed. The two men talk of Jean: in the midst of war it is wonderfully nostalgic to savour again the heartbreaks and betrayals of peacetime.

***Umfraville at Frederica's

It's a thrilling surprise to find the raffish Dicky Umfraville engaged to the notoriously strait-laced Frederica: and that she is thrilled to bits about it all. It's a perfect example of the changes war brings with it: clearly not all of them are bad.

***Robert and Flavia at Frederica's

The inclusion of Stringham's sister in the party has added spice because Umfraville, as he explains, took her virginity back in their Kenya days. His claim that he fathered Pamela in the process is regarded by Nick with scepticism. This double coincidence sets up the Feydeau-esque tour de force of the chapter's ending, which begins with Robert's news that if he can get back to his unit at once, he will be seeing action overseas.

***Arrival of Buster

Buster's arrival complicates things dreadfully. He has arrived to seek Flavia's help because his wife (her mother) has abandoned him for Norman Chandler and wants a divorce. I'm sure we have all met Busteresque upper-class sneerers who trade on social discomfort: Buster is now at tether's end and it takes a heart of stone not to laugh. As all this is going on, Odo Stevens arrives to take Nick back to the course, and continues to make good going with Priscilla.

*And Isobel goes into labour.

Nick has no option but to leave with Stevens, Robert crammed into the back of the car, like a man setting off to meet his doom.

It is, then, almost a relief to get back to calm, settled state of war, war at least as it is pursued by the army away from the front line. Once again we are short on coincidence as the narrative of Gwatkins's downfall unfolds.

*Gwylt and Maureen

Nick and Gwatkin come across Corporal Gwylt, going great guns with Gwatkin's beloved barmaid, and the awful banality of this situation is made clear for all. Gwatkin greets this with rather admirable Homeric laughter.

The volume ends with Gwatkin stripped of his company and Bithel in trouble for apparently kissing a soldier. As Nick leaves his unit there is a rare old flap on, to do with stolen butter and spoiled meat, echoing the flap that accompanies Nick's departure from Frederica's. He goes back to Div. HQ.

†****Nick is now Widmerpool's assistant.

"I felt enormously glad to see him." What can possibly go wrong? Nick's old acquaintance – no, friend – has rescued him from duties he was wholly unsuited for, and a new chapter of army life can begin. "I saw that I was now in Widmerpool's power".

The Soldier's Art

*Bithel at the air-raid

After the bravura opening with Nick's purchase of his military great-coat we are caught up in the war, at the same time frightening and dreary. The meeting with Bithel, who should have been in bed, adds a touch of ludicrousness to whole business of life, death and duty.

*Farebrother at Div. HQ

Sunny Farebrother, already mentioned at the end of the previous volume, is also part of Div. HQ. He embodies a different approach to Widmerpool: he can make people like him, and he knows how useful a weapon this is. He and Widmerpool are equally ruthless, equally interested in power and take equal delight in personal feuds.

183

†*****Stringham as waiter in F Mess

This is the most audacious and probably the least probable coincidence in the entire sequence. By the eighth volume it's safe to assume that readers who don't care for coincidence in the novel have either given up or been won over: but this is a belter, wonderfully dramatic and acceptable or not, according to taste. As usual, Powell manages it with beautiful understatement, both parties pretending ignorance of the other.

This coincidence is a startling example of what time can do to an individual: the suave, self-possessed, sardonic and melancholy figure of QU is now attempting to solve the problems of his life by seeking a romantic doom while bearing a garland of ironies. As Widmerpool manoeuvres for power, Stringham accepts his military fate, embraces his subservience: he is perhaps Vigny's military saint, as discussed by Pennistone in the previous volume. It's a startling collision between war and peace: Stringham, so magnificently perverse at Milly Andriadis's party of 1928 or 1929, now accepts the task of serving half-cooked spuds to Captain Biggs, bearing with patience his scorn and mockery. Deafy Morgan, in VB, is described as taking on his duties in a "Christ-like" way; something of the same is true of Stringham in this perfect self-abnegation. There is something beautiful here: but it it's not going to win the war.

War here is conducted without an enemy on the ground: a sense of futility dominates the exercises and the feuding. Then Jenkins gets some leave, a

184

chance to improve his military condition and to meet up with family and friends. Here Powell once again weaves a densely plotted web of coincidences. He is back in Feydeau mode once again: but as the various doors on the stage open and close, they reveal not naughtiness and frivolity but ever-more-distressing gyrations in the dance of death.

**Pennistone at the Free French

The meeting of this passing acquaintance, already halfway to becoming a friend, is a promising start to Jenkins's try-out as he seeks work in this department, but to his disappointment he isn't good enough.

*Chips at Café Royal

We are always aware of Nick's affection for Lovell, and his comments on upper-class families and their ways are as helpful to less privileged readers as they are amusing. But he's not in good shape, abandoned by Priscilla and concerned about his will: aware of mortality as everyone must in time of war.

***Audrey Maclintick at Café Royal

There is a shock at finding that Mrs Maclintick is now living with Moreland. It's clear that she has looked after him, taken him in hand, and rescued him from the disaster he was heading for in TKO. We are at once away of her good points: perhaps less reluctantly than Nick, who is inclined to dwell on her as an aspect or Moreland's "retreat from perfectionism".

***Odo Stevens and Priscilla at the Café Royal

Not too massive a coincidence, I suppose – not so many places open in wartime if you want to make something of a night of it – but his arrival brings about a great mingling of contraries. Mrs Maclintick is won over by Stevens as she was by Stringham – both characters have a lot of dash - but Priscilla is overwhelmed by the stresses of the occasion. She narrowly missed bumping into her estranged husband; now she must sit with two lovers, one current and one ex, along with her sister's husband. It's all too much and she runs for home.

***Max Pilgrim at Moreland's flat

We had already learned that Pilgrim was the lodger at the flat shared by Moreland and Mrs Maclintick: now, camp as ever (why should he not be?) he announces the death of Chips Lovell, Bijou Ardglass and the rest of her party after a bomb struck the Café Madrid. Death, thus narrated, seems sadder and more terrible than it does when couched in more conventional phrases. This is an example of Powell's use of the Unlikely Narrator.

A more conventional novel – one written by St John Clarke, perhaps, had he survived – would have had Chip's and Priscilla meeting at the Madrid just in time for the bomb to fall: a classic bit of melodrama. But Powell engineers this subtler and

186

more terrible coincidence: both dead, their situation forever unresolved, a casual double-cruelty of war.

****Nick at Lady Molly's

Faced with a duty that is as unenviable as it is unavoidable, Nick crosses London – at least, Inner London or Zone 1 as we would now call it – to South Kensington to tell Priscilla of her husband's death. But he arrives to find that another bomb has scored a direct hit on the Jeavons home: Molly and Priscilla are also dead. The awful coincidence that carried off both Chips and Pricilla on the same night has also taken Molly, who in every page she has appeared on has been full of the spirit of generosity. War is not only bloody, it is also bloody awful and bloody unfair. The narrative of war has still taken us nowhere near the front line. We have seen no actual fighting: and yet the novel is losing major characters, and well-beloved ones at that. A war that takes away Molly and leaves Ted Jeavons on his own is a very hard thing to bear.

*Stringham telephones Nick

Back at Div. HQ, Nick is called on by Stringham to help out Bithel, who is too drunk to walk. (Stringham is now serving under Bithel at the Mobile Laundry.)

**Widmerpool stumbles across Bithel and party

Rotten luck for Bithel, who had managed to delay such a disaster for far longer than expected. Widmerpool's instant vindictiveness, his total lack of sympathy or fellow-feeling, provide further revelations of Widmerpool as he really is: not only mad for power, but also revelling in pettiness. (As Gore Vidal said: "It is not enough to succeed. Others must fail.") As Widmerpool's subordinate, Nick is in the perfect position to appreciate that.

The book ends in a tightly-plotted detonation of scheming and manoeuvring between Widmerpool, Farebrother and Colonel Hogbourne-Johnson. Diplock betrays Hogbourne-Johnson's extravagant trust and deserts, Widmerpool seems on the point of losing his grand new job and Farebrother gloats, while Stringham is determined to travel to the Far East with the Mobile Laundry. We then hear that Biggs has hanged himself in the cricket pavilion.

There is a coincidence here that stretches from the previous volume: both Widmerpool and Gwatkin attempt to punish Bithel for drunkenness. Gwatkin make a terrible mess of it; Widmerpool does so with immense efficiency and unseemly relish. This is not a good moment for seeing Widmerpool's good points, even if his efficiency is to be admired.

As the volume ends Widmerpool is moving on, no matter what. Despite his earlier promise, he abandons Nick without regret. No one, it seems, gives a toss about what happens to Nick. He is apparently doomed to spend the rest of the war in ghastly, futile and totally unproductive employment. Unless a message telling him to report to the War Office changes anything.

The Military Philosophers

The next two novels are about work: professional life, its rewards and exasperations, and the extraordinary intimacy that exists between colleagues, in many ways closer than friendship. Volume 10, BDFR, is about the literary life, and Powell knows this world well enough to present it without any of the romanticism that the young Nick may feel about it in earlier volumes. But there is something a little starry-eyed about MP, which is concerned with soldiering away from the front line. There is, perhaps, the tiniest shortage of irony. Powell expects us to be as star-struck as he was by his encounters with Alanbrooke and Montgomery. Certainly both are beautifully observed, but Powell does not stand back and observe Nick's awe: he seems happy to share it.

As a result, the volume lacks a little of the edge that we have got used to in Belgravian marble halls and Fitzrovian pubs. In MP Nick is professionally fulfilled, doing a sound job, genuinely appreciated. He is overwhelmingly grateful to be doing it and making some kind of difference. All this is both understandable and admirable, but this fractional loss of detachment makes it, in my view, the weakest volume of the twelve.

Which is not to say that it isn't pretty damn good. The pattern of coincidence continues, at times devastatingly – and by the end, it is an unavoidable fact that coincidence has taken us a good way beyond naturalism.

*Cabinet Offices: Widmerpool

Nick has to go there to cover for his boss, Major Finn and his immediate boss Pennistone; we have already learnt that Widmerpool was heading in that direction ("the biggest thing of all") in the previous volume. Here we see Widmerpool at his best, in his full strength, crackling with energy and power. We get to appreciate the physical circumstances of his sinister, subterranean location, cut off from the world, cut off from ordinary people: we also see him dominate the room: he can usually "carry the meeting", as Pamela later points out. Widmerpool has come from humiliation into triumph – at last we are shown this at first hand -- but there's no temptation to rejoice for him.

**Templer at the Cabinet Offices

Templer, previously so amusing and good-natured, is thoroughly out of sorts. He is much changed, both by the war and his personal circumstances. He now comes across as rather unattractive, his life unenviable. The powerful waves of negativity that flow from him make it clear that the world is still going through terrible times, even though Nick is now a military figure of substance.

*Theodoric at War Office

A royal and an ally, a person that Nick has encountered a couple of times before, going about his business: obviously he would come in contact with Nick's department.

*Farebrother at War Office

Sonny Farebrother's new job, not quite as grand, to his chagrin, as Widmerpool's, also brings him in touch with Nick's department; Finn is at once on his guard because of Farebrother's involvement in the "secret" world. There are hints here of trouble ahead.

***Pamela as Nick's driver

Pamela is Stringham's niece. Perhaps it's not too outlandish to find an upper-class (ish) girl working as a driver at the War Office. There are hints of her involvement with Polish allies and the already notorious Szymanski.

*The Ufford as a Polish HQ

Nick realises that the semi-secret Polish HQ he visits in London was once Uncle Giles's London *pied à terre*, the Ufford. This building – like all London -- is a different place in the time of war, but it's also still the same, for nothing and no one can shake off the past. And it gives Powell a chance to repeat his joke about the Temple of Janus.

**Pamela at Ted Jeavons's party

Pamela turns up to this informal gathering as a "girlfriend" of Nora's, making it clear, after her not-quite revelations about Szymanksi, that she will play an important part in what's left of the *Dance*. In this party Pamela comes across as the most crashing bore: we have to take her infallible allure on trust. We can see for ourselves that Jean is sexy, Matty is attractive and great company and even Gipsy has her moments. But – to use that most Powellian locution – for some reason Pamela never seems – to me at least – to be someone worth bothering with, at least after the first rebuff. Is that a weakness of the novel? Powell tells us she is irresistible: for my money he doesn't really shows us. And show-don't-tell is the abiding principle of the novelist.

***Templer and Pamela

Ted gives an account of Templer's troubles, imparted to him while Templer was a lodger at his house, and explains that Pamela was at the root of them.

***Szymanski sprung from prison by Farebrother and Odo Stevens

And all this is tied in with Pamela, in a way that remains mysterious. The coincidence – we already know the plotters, Farebrother and Stevens -- asks questions of the way war should be waged, and whether conventional standards of behaviour (or for that matter morality) are of much use (or importance) when there is a war to be won. Nick, for all his Bohemian connections, is forced to abhor this outbreak of what he terms "military Bohemianism".

***Pamela and Theodoric at *The Bartered Bride*

Once again Nick is at a musical event without knowing, as Books Bagshaw remarks in another context, whether it's arseholes or Tuesday. He finds plenty of entertainment, despite his musical shortcomings, as Pam makes another appearance, this time escorted by Gwen McReith. Hard to see what brought her there, unless it was her instinct for trouble: she makes a public show of her intimacy with Theodoric, who demonstrates great sangfroid.

**Widmerpool at *The Bartered Bride*

It's not unreasonable to suppose that Widmerpool found it professionally advantageous to attend the opera, even though his musical appreciation is well below Nick's. It's here that he sees Pam in action: and is at once attracted and makes a point of finding out her name.

***Night of the flying bombs: Odo and Pam

This is the high-water mark of fear in these three war novels, and the point at which the wave of terror breaks and rolls back. The need to congregate in the hall, away from bedrooms and windows, naturally produces some odd encounters, but this one, as Nick runs into Odo and his lover Pam, is a strange one: Pam's love of destruction for its own sake is reflected in the devastation that continues outside.

†****Night of the flying bombs: Mrs Erdleigh

Stranger still that Mrs Erdleigh should turn up. If Trelawney is presented as an unambiguous though sinister fraud, Mrs Erdleigh is always someone to respect. She and Pam at once establish a mutual antipathy: they seem to understand each other on a disturbingly deep level. Mrs Erdleigh knows Pam for what she is: and Pam knows it.

*France: night in Cabourg

I'm not even sure that this counts as coincidence, though it's made to seem one by Nick's earlier Proustian musings. The night in Cabourg, in which Nick fails to notice that he is in Proust's Balbec, is an elegant tribute to another writer who wrote a roman fleuve about time, and also, by presenting this tribute in the form of coincidence, a way of expressing Powell's very different approach to the task.

***France: meeting with Kedward

Here is a brief encounter between two men who lived in suffocatingly close proximity in VB: an intimacy all but forgotten by Kedward. It's a neat tying up of ends, and an intriguing point about people who seem to obliterate the past by an act of will.

****Belgium: meeting with Bob Duport

Nick meets Duport as the war is almost ready to begin in TKO, so it's fitting that they meet again with the war almost done. Duport, too, has dallied

194

with Pam, and we learn of the death of Templer, and how his failed love affair with Pam led him to taking on this dangerous employment.

****Widmerpool's engagement to Pam

In this impossible liaison we see something of the madness of war and the wild, often hopelessly deluded ideas about how to rebuild life now the war is almost over.

***Farebrother's engagement to Tuffy

An arrangement that seems eminently suitable, after the inevitably dashing death of General Conyers, Miss Weedon's previous husband.

**Embassy party: Pam and Widmerpool quarrel

Nick meets the engaged couple at an embassy party, at which Pam picks a fight and accuses Widmerpool of murdering Templer.

*Thanksgiving Service: meeting with Widmerpool

Nick meets Widmerpool after the service and finds his self-conceit in good order. The engagement with Pam, impossibly, is still on.

*****After the Thanksgiving Service: meeting with Jean

Jean is now married to Colonel Flores, a charming and ambitious South American soldier. This is a massively unlikely encounter, but Powell tells it with his usual matter-of-fact narrative style. The sequence comes to life with the vivid charm of Colonel Flores and the faintest spark that still exists between Nick and Jean. It seems that such luxuries as nostalgia and civilised personal relationships can be taken up again. This encounter with Jean, now Señora Flores, is hard to justify as straightforward naturalism, but its improbable nature adds to the richness of the book. With that in mind -- and the magical utterances of Mrs Erdleigh still echoing from 100 pages earlier – we can think again about the power of coincidence, and how Powell's use of it as a narrative device can be understood as something not a million miles from Magical Realism.

The coincidence at the heart of this book is not, however, in the meeting of characters: it is in the implication that Widmerpool has brought about the death of both Stringham and Templer. Widmerpool sent Stringham to Singapore because he found his presence in the same establishment potentially embarrassing and/or irritating; he caused support for Temper, on assignment in the Balkans, to be withdrawn because he considered it expedient.

The justice of these implicit accusations is a matter for debate. Widmerpool could hardly have foreseen the Japanese invasion of Singapore, and for his involvement in the Templer affair we have only whispers and Pam's vindictiveness. The fact remains that Widmerpool – butt of so many of the jokes shared by Nick, Templer and Stringham in their schooldays, jokes that were part of their rituals of intimacy – has played some kind of a role in both their deaths. "That boy will be the death of me," Stringham remarks in opening chapter of the first volume. Widmerpool also spent a year of the war giving Nick hell as his immediate boss: that adds up to a wartime scoreline of 3-0 in Widmerpool's favour.

The war has been a triumph for Widmerpool: promotion, respect influence, a wife, and indisputable victory over three of his former schoolmates as well as the Germans. For Nick, the ending is more equivocal: his experience in the later part of the war has been deeply satisfying, but his future is troubling and uncertain.

****Archie Gilbert at the demob clothes store

It is gloriously fitting that Nick should meet Gilbert, the most exquisitely dressed of all the "dancing men" of the second volume, as they pick up their demob outfits and agree that they will take everything (except the underclothes). Gilbert is now married, not to a deb but a girl from "across the road" while a Gunner in North London; we are inclined to wish him good luck – and Nick too. Having won the war, they must now set out on the still harder talk of winning the peace.

Books Do Furnish a Room

This volume, perhaps more overtly than any other in the sequence, deals with the relationship between Art and Power: the tensions, compromises and contradictions that happen when they collide. In

197

these pages we are shown a series of coincidences in which Art and Power, despite their theoretical antipathy, cannot help but come together, not least because they need each other.

The novel is structured around the birth, brief life and death of the magazine *Fission* – a politico-literary publication in which art and power attempt some kind of fusion. The plot operates on the coincidence that Widmerpool gets involved. It's part of his bid for power he gets the prestige of working with – of supporting - artists; he also gets the opportunity to express his views alongside theirs. Who is exploiting whom? Is this the form of symbiosis that ecologists call mutualism?

The volume is concerned with the post-war rebuilding of ordinary life: at last there are aims other than survival. It is the chance to remake the world as it should be, however differently people see such an aim: and the act of rebuilding is at the heart of this volume.

*Short at Sillery's

Nick is at Oxford researching his book on Burton: naturally he calls on Sillery. There he bumps into the eternally colourless Short, who remains one of Sillery's great admirers.

***Ada at Sillery's

Ada, Sillery's secretary, arrives and turns out to know Pamela. She is planning to work for the new publishing house of Quiggin and Craggs, who will also publish *Fission*.

***Bagshaw on Oxford Station

Nick bumps into an old acquaintance who will go on to edit *Fission*. He is a brilliant character: the archetypal journalist, more artist than power-seeker, but fascinated by power all the same.

**Widmerpool and companions at Erridge's funeral

Here is an invasion – almost a military invasion, given Widmerpool's ostentatious about-turning – of a family occasion by the forces of left-wing politics, the forces that are now in power, to the detriment of the landed aristocracy. The party includes Quiggin, Craggs and Gypsy (now Lady Craggs), old left-wing chums of Erridge, along with Widmerpool, whom he never knew, who is there on *Fission* business. Pam has come too.

*Mona at the funeral

She might by then have been the dowager Countess of Warminster, but lacked the patience and self-abnegation to deal with Erridge – which his family rather regret. And it's always nice to hear from Mona.

*Quiggin offers Nick a job at *Fission*

Though not without making it clear that Nick is at best third choice and that his family connections (Erridge has left money for the use of the publishing house and its magazine) are more important than his ability.

*Meeting with Moreland

Nicks bumps into Moreland in the street on the way to *Fission*; no plot-point but it keeps Moreland in play and it's always nice to hear from him as well, and to enjoy his views on the Moderns and the post-war generation.

***Fission* party: Odo

Odo Stevens arrives, unexpectedly working as assistant for Mark Members and his cultural organisation. We never learn how this came about. He makes a bee-line for Rosie Manasch, also a backer of *Fission*.

Fission party: Trapnel meets Widmerpool

Trapnel first ingratiates himself with Widmerpool and then borrows a quid: art forced to abase itself in front of power, convinced it will have the last laugh.

Fission party: Trapnel meets Pamela

And it was loathing at first sight for both of them. The party ends with Trapnel getting into a taxi with a flourish: his story in the place of honour in the magazine, he has cut a dash at the party, and he can consider himself to have gone one-up on both the Widmerpools.

*Dinner with Roddy Cutts at the House of Commons: meeting with Widmerpool

No great coincidence, since Widmerpool and Cutts are both MPs. Perhaps we should note here that in this volume (and most others) left-wingers are observed with plenty of irony (Erridge, Bagshaw, Sillery, Quiggin etc.), but Cutts, a successful Tory politician, is no less a comic figure.

***Pamela leaves Widmerpool

The coincidence is not Pamela's departure but that Nick (and Cutts) are there to witness the moment when Short (Widmerpool's neighbour) breaks the news to Widmerpool. This is not a coincidence of the magical, the Trelawneyesque, the Einsteinian variety. Rather it is a coincidence of the plot-builder: a useful, even essential, but always slightly artificial device. Powell avoids this kind of coincidence as far as he can – and we will see in the next volume how three potential plot-builder's coincidences are avoided by virtuoso novel-writing skills – but here is a beautifully realised but unsubtle coincidence: the narrator who just happens to be there at the crucial moment. A further example of this follows hard-upon. But in this instance, we get the full measure of things; Widmerpool's self-conceit in tatters, Pam's recklessness, and the fact that her lover is none other than Trapnel. It is a triumph of the artists over the power-seekers: and it is frighteningly brief, if not entirely illusory.

****Widmerpool visits Trapnel and Pam

And once again, Nick just happens to be there at the crucial moment. He has two good reasons for doing so: professionally, as the editor of *Fission's* book pages, and personally, since he has accepted that Trapnel as an artist who (1) needs support and (2) is worth the trouble. All that is fine and wholly believable. But the timing – well, it requires a certain willingness to accept the novel's conventions and suspend disbelief.

Is Powell pushing his luck here? It's a question that would interest Trapnel when he discusses the Heresy of Naturalism in the next chapter. How far you can push coincidence in the pursuit of a plot? How much further you can push coincidence when you go beyond naturalism and imbue coincidence with a certain amount of magic?

In the confrontation with Widmerpool, Trapnel seeks mastery of the situation and fails. He is out-faced and outmanoeuvred, his art and his dedication to his art provoking only contempt. Widmerpool even stands up to Trapnel's histrionics with his unsheathed sword: facing down Trapnel with more composure than we might have expected. Perhaps his contempt has given him strength. Certainly he stands there brushing his hat, unshakably convinced of his superiority to Trapnel and all his works: and for that matter, the superiority of his chosen way of life to that of all artists.

†*Trapnel finds his drowned manuscript

Not all that much of a coincidence, since Pamela threw the manuscript of Trapnel's novel *Profiles in String* in the canal just where he was most likely to see it. But it is a chance encounter nonetheless.

Perhaps only a fellow-novelist can appreciate the true horror of this event. It is the theft of a life. A novel can never be re-written in the same way, any more than a life can be re-lived. The implication is that *Profiles in String* would have been a very good novel indeed, and that Trapnel's life would have been forever changed by its reception, author of an acknowledged masterpiece. Pam removes from Trapnel the entire point of being Trapnel: and she does so in a manner calculated to make this loss as public and as painful as possible.

It is at this point that you can understand the union of Mr and Mrs Widmerpool. They have united to destroy Trapnel. Both have celebrated the power they wield, in their very different spheres: and together they have prevailed over art. The post-war years will not see the building of a New Jerusalem in England, a civilisation based on truth and art and beauty. The same old values will prevail in different form.

Trapnel's novel is drowned, *Fission* had gone the way of all magazines, which is a sadness to any writer who might have placed a piece there, and the Widmerpools are in charge.

*Meeting with Le Bas

Not a great stretch, since Nick is visiting his old school and Le Bas is still there: they discuss the various fates of the Nick's school contemporaries: and Le Bas, inks a precise circle around the name of Widmerpool.

***Meeting with Widmerpool outside the school

The events of the novel seem to have taken it out of Widmerpool as he sits on the wall outside the school gates waiting for Pamela, who is visiting one of the boys, for reasons we don't go into, perhaps something of a relief.

This was Widmerpool's big chance. The post-war years, the rebuilding years, the years on which the Labour government changed so much: this was the opportunity for Widmerpool to go big, to seize real power, to become the figure he had always imagined himself to be in his awkward, sweating, hard-running schooldays: a power in the land, a person who made his mark on history.

But his career seems even at this point to have missed its trajectory. Perhaps he needed *Fission* (and its attendant artists) more than he thought. Perhaps he didn't fit in with the Labour party any more than he fitted in at school. Either way we leave him at the end of this volume sitting glumly (like Humpty Dumpty) on a wall, waiting on the convenience of a wife who's taste for devastation goes way beyond the destruction of mere artists. In this volume Widmerpool has won: and as Pyrrhus said after the battle of Asculum, another victory like that and we are done for.

Temporary Kings

You could visit most of the locations in the *Dance* up to this point with a London Zone 1 Travelcard. There is of course the occasional weekend in the country, two trips to France and the army postings in Wales and Northern Ireland: but these apart, you could make a pretty comprehensive *Dance* pilgrimage on foot in half a day.

But in a drastic break with the established pattern we leap 11 years into the future and arrive in Venice, where more than half the book's action takes place. Neither Wales nor Ireland impose greatly on the action in those first two wartime novels, but Venice can't help but make its presence felt. Here the stage itself always takes centre-stage – and Venice is the great city of coincidence.

Once, when I was visiting the Scuola di San Giorgio and its Carpaccios, I was asked to sign the visitor's book. On the same page, three spaces above the one in which I was to write, I found the name of a former love. Inevitably, we met when crossing a campo in opposite directions. I used this encounter as the starting point for a short story: those few that read it said the coincidence was too far-fetched. They were right: truth is no defence in libel or naturalistic fiction. It was true but it didn't *feel* true: useless to point out that for the visitor to Venice the fantastic is the stuff of everyday life. Venice is the city of coincidence.

Trelawneyesque coincidences are obligatory here: the layout of the city, with its canals and its bridges, is like a scientific diagram representing the mechanism of coincidence. Coincidence is too easy here: so Powell, at least at first, reins himself in. He begins by introducing two new characters, Emily Brightman and Russell Gwinnett.

***Gwinnet announces himself Trapnel's biographer

Though we seem to be setting off in new direction, we never leave or wish to break free from the underlying pattern of the *Dance*: like a set of musical variations the underlying theme, though it appears to be constantly changing, is inescapable and always the same. Gwinnett, a new character from the New World, is working on a biography of the archetypally English figure X Trapnel: clearly what matters is the universal, rather than the local significance of Trapnel's oeuvre.

We then have a flash-back to Trapnel's death. Nick wasn't there: instead he recounts through the reports of different eye-witnesses, who see it from different vantage-points with different kinds of understanding. This is a bravura rejection of the Authorial Coincidences of BDFR: a device that you might call Coincidence Avoidance. Here Powell produces us a kind of cubistic narrative: giving different possibilities of the story all at the same time. It is wonderfully skilful in the purely technical sense, bringing in other characters known to readers from earlier volumes. Powell is so taken with this method that he uses it twice more in the same volume: in the story of Pam's naked appearance at the Bagshaw house and yet again with the street scene after the Mozart party. Each one is so brilliantly executed that you have no problem with the repetitive nature of the device: it's all of a piece with Nick's role of observer, listener and reporter.

***Newspaper report of the death of Ferrand-Seneschal

This brings Pamela back into the narrative, for the report implies that she was with Ferrand-Seneschal at his death: *L'après midi d'un monstre*. Dr Brightman knows that Pamela is in Venice. The coincidence trap has been baited: now it must be sprung.

**Tiepolo: Pamela and Glober

As Nick goes to view the great Tiepolo ceiling with Gwinnett and Dr Brightman, he comes across Pamela. He also finds Louis Glober (another New Worlder), already introduced by way of a flashback in the previous chapter. Gwinnett meets Pamela: at once, and rather surprisingly, she seems willing to help him with his Trapnel researches. Since both the oeuvre and the biographical material available to Gwinnett are thin, this is make or break

for the biographer. Gwinnett meets this challenge
head-on.

***Tiepolo: arrival of Widmerpool

The timing of Widmerpool's arrival is a fairly
hefty coincidence: and it puts the ingredients together
for a series of heavyweight interactions. These begin
as Pamela, who had for once been in a relatively
agreeable frame of mind, shifts into a reckless attack
on her husband, taunting him, deliberately
withholding from him vital information and mocking
his sexual tastes in front of a captive audience.

*Biennale: Ada and Glober

Nick visits the biennale with his former boss
Daniel Tokenhouse, who has already been subtly
introduced to us in the earlier flashback about
Glober's visit to London, so the visit feels part of the
pattern of coincidence. They run into Ada and Glober,
a straightforward Venetian coincidence, have a boozy
lunch together and go back to Tokenhouse's flat to
view his work.

*****Widmerpool at Tokenhouse's flat

Here it becomes clear – or rather, it becomes
slightly less murky – that Widmerpool is involved in
some kind of clandestine activity and that Tokenhouse
is also concerned. Tokenhouse, a disaffected leftward-
leaning Brit, is willing to do small services for people
and also for a theory of government he admires. He
has neither loyalty nor admiration for Widmerpool,

208

but is apparently obliged to help him out. Widmerpool is in a bad way: agitated, involved in something, in above his head. It seems he is no longer seeking power by the front door – by becoming a minster or a colonial governor or a great industrialist – but by intrigue and covert dealings. He certainly doesn't share Tokenhouse's idealism. The meeting seems – though in this matter nothing is certain – to show Widmerpool as not only nasty but treasonous, and not only treasonous but incompetently so.

A few pages later Ada is telling Nick about a further shocking scene involving Pamela, and that Glober, stout fellow, is planning to marry Pamela. The tide is turning against Widmerpool.

**Nick and Gwinnett meet Rosie and Odo Stevens at Florian's

Sit long enough at Florian's and you'll meet someone you know. This chance meeting sets things up for

*Pam's arrival at Florian's

She tells us more about Widmerpool's plight, accompanies Nick and Gwinnet as they walk out of the piazza and stages a little scene in Trapnel's memory. To her fury Gwinnett is profoundly unimpressed, but as she hurries away, he chases after her. Something's going on: no one is quite sure what.

*Bagshaw offers to take on Gwinnett

We're back in London, Zone 2 to be accurate and Primrose Hill. Bagshaw's eagerness to accept Gwinnett as a paying guest – the opportunity for Trapnel conversations is no doubt agreeable to both parties - is tidy in terms of plotting, and makes it possible for the story of Pamela's late night naked visit to Gwinnet to be told from its various points of view. It's still not clear what's going on: only that Pamela, like her husband, is losing control.

**Reunion dinner: Cheeseman

Reunion dinners are specifically designed to bring about chance meetings and collisions between the past and the present. This is why Powell uses them a fair bit, and also why he apologises for them – "not far from a vice". In this one Cheesman, former commander of the Mobile Laundry, turns up unexpectedly and gives hints of the horrors endured as a prisoner of war under the Japanese, and of Stringham's courage in these circumstances. Stringham has, in a quiet way, died a hero. For some reason we are glad to hear that: he is, after all, one of the most engaging characters in the *Dance*.

**Mozart party: Moreland and Audrey Maclintick

It turns out that Moreland has been advising anonymously on the production of the opera: his appearance contributes to the complex mix of characters at the event. But his most significant contribution is his part in the multi-voice narrative of the street-scene at the evening's end. Audrey is shown for once in a sympathetic light, fussing affectionately over Moreland.

***Mozart party: the Widmerpools

What on earth persuaded the Widmerpools to come to this party? Their host Short may well be a great Mozartian, but the only piece of music Widmerpool has ever praised is The Merry Widow Waltz, while the only aesthetic opinion Pamela has ever expressed is the inadequacy of Trapnel's masterpiece. It's suggested that Widmerpool took this opportunity to show himself at what Moreland calls "a fashionable event", to make it clear to the world he was rising above his troubles. Or perhaps (this possibility is not ventilated in the narrative) Pamela knew that Glober and Polly Duport were planning to come and relished the confrontation.

**Mozart party: Glober and Polly

Glober has pulled back from the idea of marrying Pamela and making her star in a film based on Trapnel's life and work; instead he arrives with the already well-established film star Polly Duport, Jean's daughter. It's a party and a classy bit of culture: a reasonable enough place for Glober, and besides, Polly knows the hostess, Rosie.

**Mozart party: Carolo

Here is a peripheral, almost a decorative coincidence: Carolo turns up as a replacement violinist; he is a former husband of Matilda and the man for whom Audrey Maclintick left her husband.

*Mozart party: Matilda

Matilda also arrives: it's as if two of her former husbands (Carolo and Moreland) have combined to put on this divertissement to please her; she graciously accepts Carolo's bow. She has chosen Power rather than Art, and it seems to suit her.

†***Mozart party: Mrs Erdleigh and Stripling

Surprising to see this couple at a musical evening, but Stripling is a crony of Odo's, bonding over vintage cars. Perhaps Mrs Erdleigh has an unrevealed taste for opera. This reckless mixture of people attending the Mozart party makes possible the violent street-scene that follows. It begins when Pamela confronts Glober and Polly.

It's here that Mrs Erdleigh steps in to warn Pamela of the horrors that lie ahead. Her "rays of mystic disapproval" define the complex scene: as expounded mostly by Stevens and Moreland, whose contrasting understanding of what is happening make the events so vivid. Moreland's grasp of Mrs Erdleigh's possibilities light up the scene and turn it into a formal struggle between good and evil. Pamela's hostility to life and love seems to reveal something deeper and far worse than an incipient breakdown.

There are many touches of the supernatural in the pages of the *Dance*: Mrs Erdleigh's fortune-telling, planchette, the Stonehurst ghost, Dr Trelawney's pronouncements and Mrs Erdleigh's earlier encounter with Pamela. Here they all come together. It's possible to keep an open mind about paranormal activities, but not about evil. Mrs Erdleigh makes that quite clear.

The violence that follows is mild, but it adds to our realisation that people have stepped beyond the conventions of public behaviour. All restraint has been lost. Widmerpool is hooshed away in Short's delayed car, broken glasses and all: Pamela, not inappropriately, has vanished into the night, never to be seen again.

*Widmerpool on Westminster Bridge

This chance encounter, at no great stretch of plausibility, sets the seal on the strange events that have taken place, and does so in the context of Moreland's wistful and touching deathbed scene. Some mysteries are now slightly less opaque: we learn the tiniest bit more about Pamela's death and the most discreet and well-mannered act of necrophilia in the history of literature.

***Vintage cars: Glober, Stripling and Odo

As Nick and Widmerpool talk, the vintage cars pass: Moreland had been fascinated by the passions they excite in their enthusiasts. Now we see them in reality, piloted by those who had played a part in the same post-Mozart street scene.

Why vintage cars? Perhaps because we can never escape the past even as we run pell-mell into the future, or perhaps because passion is always ludicrous, whether it's Widmerpool's passion for Pamela – and for that matter, Glober's and Odo's - or Stripling's passion for cars. Whatever else it is, passion is an irrefragable sign of being alive.

Widmerpool stands on the bridge, apparently in ruins. Nick makes his excuses and leaves, no longer willing to be part of this. Widmerpool walks on across the bridge, in the opposite direction to the flow of vintage cars.

Hearing Secret Harmonies

A long series of coincidences has brought us so far: now we must get through to the end. We will do so in a Bonfire Night of coincidences: a detonation of blazing fireworks that seem to set the air itself on fire before vanishing as if they had never. Now coincidence will pile on top of coincidence, naturalism in the Trapnel sense more and more set aside, till the inextricable combination of mundanity and magic finally runs its course and Nick stands alone in his garden as the flames of his own bonfire take a hold on the items gathered together for sacrifice.

*Fiona and the caravan

But we begin, as the previous volume did, with a new location and new characters: as if coincidence was the last thing on the author's mind. A small favour to a junior relative is part of the routine of family life: Nick's niece Fiona arrives with her fellow cult-members and their leader, Scorp Murtlock. In the course of the afternoon Murtlock reveals his taste for mysticism, mystification and mastery: and also apparently reveals a genuine paranormal gift as he announces the whereabouts of Mr Gauntlett's missing dog. Only Mrs Erdleigh has been credited with similar feats of divination.

*St John Clarke television programme

No great stretch to have a programme devoted to a once-important novelist: unsurprisingly it involves many old friends: the Quiggins, Members. Guggenbuhl (now Gainsborough).

***Widmerpool on the news

A university parade seems an odd occasion for a newsreel camera crew, but they certainly got an acceptable little scoop: Widmerpool, the new chancellor, paint-bombed and then making an excited statement to camera. We later learn that the Quiggin twins, daughters to JG and Ada, are responsible for the attack. Must have been a slow news day.

*Magnus Donners Prize

This is a neat device to bring various characters together: Donners's widow Matilda has set it up, using as bait for Nick the photos of the seven deadly sins from TKO: a sudden shaft of nostalgia of the kind that laid Moreland out at the Mozart party. Norman Chandler turns up to view them. As the dealings with the prize continue, we have Emily Brightman and Members as Nick's fellow-judges, and the introduction of Delavacquerie as secretary.

***Sunny Farebrother on the tube

A chance meeting with Farebrother, who has been to the funeral of Jimmy Stripling: he reveals that Stripling was involved with a mystic group that sounds like Murtlock's lot, though this is never confirmed. Farebrother admires their leader's organising ability. It's also clear that Stripling's death has created a vacancy for a reasonably wealthy backer; you have to admire Powell's thoroughness when it comes to plotting a novel.

*Gwinnett wins Magnus Donners prize

And that thoroughness is shown again when the judges find themselves in agreement: Gwinnett's book about Trapnel must get the prize. Nick is not surprised that the book is good, only that it is finished. I am astonished that he managed to complete it without using the name Widmerpool; it seems that Gwinnett as author possesses talents for evasiveness that Powell himself would envy. How did it read? False name? Well-chosen formula? Every author knows that avoidance of a name is not enough to avoid a libel action. How did Gwinnett pull this off?

216

Perhaps it's a task for the Anthony Powell Society's practitioners of metafiction.

***Widmerpool at the dinner for the Magnus Downers Prize

The dinner naturally and inevitably brings many familiar characters together, including Widmerpool. His involvement with the prize, through financial responsibilities given to him years ago by Donners himself, has given him a certain power over the situation. He uses the occasion for a harangue about the need to destroy society.

****Quiggin twins at the Magnus Donner Prize Dinner

The involvement of the Quiggin twins as star items of Widmerpool's collection of rebellious young people is pushing it a little, but we can take it in stride. But how does Widmerpool persuade them to come to the dinner? The 60s was a time when living gurus and leaders were eagerly sought: Tariq Ali, Timothy Leary, Abbie Hoffman, John Lennon, Maharishi Mahesh Yogi. Widmerpool wishes to be among them, and Amanda and Belinda are disciples.

He has made himself an authority figure for anti-authoritarianism. This was a time when many people were seeking a new and better world, and many leaders were tried and found wanting: a trend summed up in the post-60s song by The Who: *Won't Get Fooled Again*.

At the dinner the twins reinforce Widmerpool's speech of destruction by letting off fireworks and a stink-bomb before escaping, leaving Widmerpool gasping in admiration. "That was a happening if you like."

***Widmerpool at Royal Academy dinner

Here is a good occasion for chucking lots of people together: the older guests in tails and orders and the younger in "knock about the studio" garb. Nick comes across as a bit of a crusty old bugger at this point, a side mostly suppressed by his genuine interest in other people, no matter what their ages or affiliations. The surprise is that Widmerpool turns up, no great enthusiast for the visual arts (or any other kind).

**Canon Fenneau at the RA dinner

Here is a virtuoso coincidence: the silent Paul from Sillery's tea-party in the first volume returns after an absence of ten volumes to sit opposite Nick. By a still greater coincidence he is an expert on Scorp Murtlock. He makes the link between Murtlock and Trelawney: at once Murtlock becomes a more sinister figure.

***Widmerpool meets Fenneau

Widmerpool makes himself known to Fenneau with the aim of making contact with Murtlock. Fenneau issues a warning which Widmerpool brushes off. Fenneau then reveals to

Nick that Murtlock is seeking Widmerpool, and the crucial coming-together of the plot is established with very little strain on probability. Fenneau himself points out: "To those familiar with the rhythm of living there are few surprises in this world." Murtlock and Widmerpool are both seeking power through the 60s counter-culture: each has something the other wants.

****The dance at the Devil's Fingers

The convenient location of the ancient monument, the Devil's Fingers, has already been established in the opening chapter of HSH. It is ideal for Murtlock and his cult: unguarded, unenclosed, secluded and yet reasonably easy of access. Nick hears about mysterious doings up there from Mr Gauntlett: naked dancers and mysterious lights. This prepares the ground for the next and more startling coincidence.

†****Meeting with Gwinnett; his exposition of the doings at the Devil's Fingers.

Gwinnett's fascination with Murtlock's cult can't be entirely explained as legitimate research on Gothic symbols of mortality. He is well-established as a deeply peculiar man, who, with his shaven head, has now come to look like the death's head symbol on Trapnel's cane.

Gwinnett's involvement makes it possible for us to hear about the dance, the sexual invocations, the knife-fight and the retreat down the hillside. It's clear

219

that this was a struggle for power, but -- at least superficially -- it's all very different from Widmerpool's earlier more humdrum power-seeking through business, the army, literature, politics and clandestine dealings. Murtlock is seeking nothing less than power over life and death. This must always end in failure, but perhaps blaming Widmerpool is an important gain for Murtlock.

***Delvacquerie and Fiona

Delvacquerie turns out to have tendresse for Fiona, his son's former girlfriend. As a result we learn more about the cult and its doings.

Stourwater wedding

The venue for the wedding receptions is itself a fine coincidence. The decision to get married is, as Powell says earlier, a violent assertion of the will, an attempt to seize control of time future: but Stourwater is also full of powerful memories of things past for Nick. And a family wedding is always going to bring plenty of old friends together.

**Flavia Wisebite

Flavia – Stringham's sister, Pamela's mother – is the bride's godmother. She is Widmerpool's former mother-in-law, reminding us that he lives locally, along with Murtlock's cult, local celebrities. She has had a life with little enough love in it: the high spot apparently her time with Dicky Umfraville in Kenya all those years ago. Dicky, present at the wedding as a family member, escapes from this uncomfortable meeting, and after a while, Nick does the same, thoroughly out of sorts after listening to her sad tale in the context of Stourwater's insistent past.

***Gwinnett and Fiona as married couple.

As Nick has a tramp round the castle remembering the Seven Deadly Sins and other pleasantly disturbing moments, he bumps into Gwinnett and Fiona: Fiona has not only escaped from Murtlock but also from Delavacquerie. She seems to be someone people like to annex. She and Gwinnett seem rather sweet together: Nick reflects that "if he had done some dubious things in his time, so had she". That is, I supposed, a fairly mild summary of necrophilia and necromantic rites involving multiple sexual couplings, but even in such sensational events, Powell remains wedded to the power of understatement.

*Arrival of the Cult

The three of them step outside the castle, and with easy inevitability, the Cult is passing by, taking an afternoon run under the supervision of Widmerpool rather than Murtlock. Fiona reveals her taste for mischief by seeking them out and inviting them to the wedding reception: one more mixing of disparate and irreconcilable elements.

*****Bithel

60s cults often aimed to be something more than the whim or fancy of the young: offering not an adjunct of fashion but an eternal truth from which all ages could benefit. The backing or support of people other than young hippies added a depth and meaning to the concern: which helps to explain Murtlock's need for "an aged man" among his disciples, as well as his apparent importance in various rituals.

But the fact that this aged man turns out to be Bithel is remarkable, startling, dramatic: utterly compelling of the attention. Bithel, last reported weeping as Widmerpool dismissed him from the army, and before that insensible in the helping arms of Nick and Stringham, now turns up as a cult member. Widmerpool lets slip some of the effects his arrival had on the cult: it prompted a drastic shift of power, making way for Widmerpool's total subjection to Murtlock by way of a series of exacting penances.

Bithel laid bare the more ludicrous side of the army, the fallible nature of the machine and of the individuals who make it up. He adds an eerie dignity to the cult as we meet them in the course of their run: a man who has severed connection with realities as most of us understand them. He is suborned by Fiona to come and mingle with the wedding guests, the rest follow, with Widmerpool and Nick still trying feebly to stop them.

**Widmerpool and Akworth

The bride, Clare Akworth, is granddaughter to Bertram Akworth, who is known to Nick by reputation; he was expelled from school for sending a love-note to Templer, intercepted and reported by Widmerpool. So much has already been explained. Akworth's presence at the wedding has filled Widmerpool with holy zeal: he wants to make a public apology to Akworth: Akworth's youthful desire for Templer should be shared and celebrated.

As a way of disrupting a well-mannered upper-class wedding it could hardly be bettered: and it's perhaps a shame for readers that Widmerpool makes a mess of it. But such extravagances are not Powell's way: once again he refuses to take the St John Clarke route. Once again Powell presents a major event as an internal drama, instantaneous and sensational, played out to an audience of one. Nick is the only who knows what Widmerpool is up to, and Flavia's sudden indisposition takes all the limelight away from Widmerpool's self-abasement.

***Chuck's intervention

It turns out that Barnabas's former boyfriend Chuck is at the wedding, as he is a driver in the bride's advertising agency and (we learn later) has always wanted to wear a grey tail-coat. He makes his stand: Barnabas can consider himself rescued.

*Murtlock's arrival

Murtlock turns up to discipline his straying flock: his arrival over the field is beautifully told in terms of the arrival of the monster Apollyon in *Pilgrim's Progress*. It's also the arrival of the headmaster into an unruly dormitory: all the fun vanishing in an instant. He learns that Barnabas is planning to leave, and takes this without apparent concern. But then Widmerpool himself decides that he too has had enough, he must go, get out somehow, the cult can have the cottage, all his money or most of it, anything, he just has to leave.

Murtlock utterly forbids this. And it is clear at once that this is a decision of utter finality: after all, the 12-volume sequence has only a single short chapter to go: we can feel the scanty weight of these pages in our right hand hands as we turn yet another page.

*

Every story ever plotted is based, at least to an extent, on coincidence. In Graham Greene's *Travels With My Aunt* Aunt August tells an excellent story based on a double-coincidence and explains: "I sometimes believe in a Higher Power, even though I am a Catholic."

The plotting of coincidence requires great skill and judgment: it must be plausible or at least acceptable, to place Nick and Stringham together at the same mess in Ulster, or to bring Bithel and Nick together outside a castle 30 years later. Plot construction is not something critics get excited about, certainly not in literary fiction, preferring to tell us what the book Really Means. No one explains how adroitly plotted were the near-misses and eventual meeting of Bloom and Stephen in *Ulysses*, only their payload of symbolism.

But plotting is a lofty skill: far more than the plumbing and engineering of a novel. Those who think plotting is a small deal compared to more highfalutin virtues should try and write a novel in the style of JK Rowling or PG Wodehouse.

Should we add the name of Anthony Powell to this august pair of plotters? I think so. After all, Powell can bring Widmerpool and Nick to Lady Molly's on the same evening along with Widmerpool's fiancée; he can bring the Morelands and the Templers together in a sinful romp at Stourwater; he can bring Dr Trelawney and Mrs Erdleigh to attend the death of Uncle Giles.

But as we head into the very last chapter of the 12-volume sequence, it grieves me to point out a couple of small plot-holes, places at which the machinery of coincidence breaks down, or at least fails to operate with its customary smoothness.

****The Deacon Retrospective at the Barnabas Henderson Gallery

Here is an enthralling double-coincidence: Mr Deacon's paintings are in favour at last and it's Barnabas who makes it possible. These paintings, roundly derided by Nick at the start of volume two, are now Great Art. Tastes and mores have changed. By the 1970s Deacon's subject-matter might almost be considered almost mainstream. Homosexuality was newly legal and could be celebrated on the walls of the committed and the daring. The word "gay", meaning homosexual, was even then almost respectable: here was a painter and an exhibition perfectly suited to changing times.

There is a comic misunderstanding between Nick and Henderson when Nick arrives at the gallery: Henderson refuses to believe that Nick can have known Mr Deacon. But a few minutes later, Norman Chandler has arrived full of banter and stories about Mr Deacon. He is clearly on the best of terms with Barnabas, and nor is it his first visit to the show: it's inconceivable that Barnabas wasn't aware that "Bosworth Deacon" was also Edgar, friend, perhaps more than friend of Chandler and therefore known to Nick.

All the same, it's glorious to see Deacon Unbound: to celebrate the notion that his art has survived time, calumny and rejection – and that Henderson can bring about this rescue not long after his own rescue from the Murtlock cult. Though I should also point out that Barnabas's hard-sell technique is not something you will find at any smart gallery: the people who work in such places are trained, for example, never to ask, "Can I help you?" – which is too easily interpreted as "piss off".

The Duport Collection

Duport's collection of Victorian seascapes is also on sale in this apparently quite extensive gallery. But when did Duport collect them? It was Mr

Templer, father of Peter and Jean, who is first shown as an enthusiast for such pictures in QU; they are remarked on a second time when they turn up in Peter's Maidenhead house, again not related to Duport. The only reference to Duport's visual taste is at Molly Andriadis's party (at a house she rents from the Duports) in ABM: "The pictures! My God, the pictures," as the character, later revealed as Pennistone, points out.

But it seems that Mr Templer's paintings have become the Duport Collection. Perhaps Duport took them on after Mr Templer's death, perhaps as a result collecting more, or perhaps he already had a taste for Victorian seascapes. Either way, it's unexplained: and therefore a slightly untidy loose end. I point this out not from the glee at doing so, but rather, to point out how few loose ends there are in this vast scheme of coincidence.

****Arrival of Chandler, Jean, Duport and Polly

An unexpected meeting that ramps up what Moreland would no doubt agree were the already alarming nostalgic possibilities of this visit: Duport, once a hated and feared enemy, is now immensely affable, while the once beloved Jean denies Nick (but did he seek it?) a farewell kiss.

****Bithel's arrival

It's plausible that Bithel should arrive, since Henderson has made a point of staying in touch with him. It's stretching things that Nick should happen to

227

be there, staying after the gallery closed for the night to hear Henderson's story: Nick's passion for gossip – for information about the intimate doings of the people around him – is unabated after half a century and getting on for a million words.

Bithel arrives in a terrible state, sobered up by a quarter-bottle of Scotch in jig-time, and he is there to play the part of the messenger, in the manner of the slave who tells the story of the blinding of King Oedipus. But here, for this is Powell, everything is in a minor key and played on muted and perhaps inappropriate instruments. The comic nature of Bithel's stumbling narrative brings out the ludicrous nature of Widmerpool's death, the terrible solemnity of Widmerpool's death and the comic, solemn and terrible ending of this immense sequence of interlocking stories and coincidences.

**The Modigliani

One last moment, one final coincidence. Widmerpool is dead, Pam is dead, Stringham is dead, but the Modigliani drawing has survived, and Bithel is its unlikely saviour. We have seen the drawing briefly at Stringham's flat, we hear of its removal from Widmerpool's flat as Pam elopes with Trapnel, we see it over the mantelpiece at their bivouac in Little Venice. Now it appears once again, this time as the penultimate symbol and the last coincidence: a piece of simple and perfect beauty.

228

Afterword

Earlier in the final volume Delavacquerie makes a throwaway remark: "Love and Literature should rank before Sorcery and Power." The capped-up words make it clear that this is quite a significant statement. You could, if you like, take this what you might call "the message" of the *Dance* -- and then try and work out which side won.

But I'm not inclined to dwell there too long. Jean-Luc Godard, asked about the meaning of one of his films, replied: "*Le moral, c'est le travelling*;" that is to say, the moral is the tracking-shots. Or that the meaning of the film and its technique are inextricable. I am inclined to think so far as the *Dance* is concerned, *le moral c'est le coincidence*: that this pattern of coincidence is not just how the sequence is put together but what it actually means. Reading is not about getting through to the end so you can work out the meaning: it is about the experience of reading: *le travelling*, no less. When Widmerpool is engaged to Mildred Haycock, and so future brother-in-law to General Conyers, Nick muses: "I attempted to find some parallel, however far-fetched, to link Widmerpool with General Conyers, thereby hoping to construct one of those formal designs in human behaviour which for some reason afford an obscure satisfaction to the mind: making the apparent inconsistencies of life easier to bear."

Alas, the comparison soon breaks down. The great dance of coincidence that we witness across all 12 volumes seems at times to create a formal pattern

229

of human behaviour, but then it breaks down and we must look for the next coincidence to try and make sense of things, knowing that in the end there is no sense and no pattern: only coincidence: and coincidence is the meaning and the moral of *A Dance to the Music of Time*.

By the end of the 12 volumes nothing remains of Widmerpool but a few memories of those who knew him. He dies, it seems, as unloved as he had lived, as unloving as he was unlovable. At least the Modigliani was saved from the funeral pyre.

The book began in fire, with the brazier that glowed by the side of the road on a snowy evening; now it must end in fire as Nick sets a match to a garden bonfire... and for some reason even the formal measure of coincidence seems suspended as the smoke begins to rise.

The Snob Thing

We know better than to talk about Anthony Powell among strangers, or even among quite good friends. We wish at all costs to avoid the Snob Conversation: Anthony Powell is not worth reading because he's a snob. That's why I've never actually read him. Thus the non-reader is shown to be more literate and discerning than the reader.

And admittedly, a mildly antipathetic reading of the opening volume is not going to allay such fears in superficial readers: Eton, even if not named, is followed by lunch at the Stringhams' town house near Berkeley Square and an alarming encounter with Buster; after that we move on to "the" university, surely the most snobbish way possible of referring to Oxford.

So let's work out what people mean by snobbery in a writer. Is it a tendency to write about people of privileged background? Is it snobbish to choose lords and ladies as your subject matter? If that's the case, Shakespeare, who wrote about kings, is even more of a snob than Powell, while Homer, who wrote about gods, is the biggest snob of all.

Would-be writers are always being told to write – at least at first – of what they know. A white male middleclass writer attempting a naturalistic novel probably won't choose to write about the rap artists of Brixton or the domestic life of women in Southall or family life in the favelas of São Paolo, not from snobbery but from shortage of relevant experience. If you went to Eton you'd probably write more vividly about Eton than Tulse Hill Comprehensive. Besides, choice of subject is not what makes a novel good or bad: it's what the novelist does with it.

So let's define snobbery – social snobbery – as valuing well-born (and/or wealthy) people more highly than the rest: so the snobbish writer writes as if people with titles and money were by definition more interesting, valuable and worthwhile than those who lack them. A snob is instinctively obsequious to superiors and contemptuous of perceived inferiors, in the manner of Captain Cocksidge.

It you accept that, you must also agree that Powell is by no means the champion literary snob. Proust beats him hands-downs, most especially in the volume *The Guermantes Way* in which the narrator, at least for a while, sees his own social climbing as the legitimate pursuit of all meaning and happiness.

Evelyn Waugh's *Brideshead Revisited* is about a man's life-altering bedazzlement by an aristocratic family. Members of this family, the Flytes, are set against the boorish but bewildered Canadian millionaire Rex Mottram, fiancé and later husband of Julia Flyte. He doesn't get the hang of them at all – but Charles the narrator does, and that flatters us readers and draws us into a conspiracy against Rex. The sequence in which he and Charles dine together in Paris is one of the most outrageously snobbish pieces of writing in all literature. "The sole was so simple and unobtrusive that Rex failed to notice it."

But the next thing to say is that these are both great novels; Proust in the very front rank, Waugh not a million miles behind. To be snobbish doesn't necessarily make you a bad novelist. Good novelists often – and great writers always -- write better than they know or intend.

Anyone is entitled not to like a novel, or the entire body of work of any novelist. It's a free library, after all. The greatest literary critics in history can't actually *prove* that that Proust is better than Powell, or for that matter, Ian Fleming. Henry James may be one of the greatest writers that ever drew breath but I've never got on with him. My loss, I know: one that exposes the limitations not of the writer but of the reader.

You are entitled to dislike any book for whatever capricious reason you choose. Powell talks somewhere about people who can't read Conrad because they don't like novels about the sea. You can dislike all Russian novels because the names are trying. You can dislike Vikram Seth's *An Equal Music* because you hate "classical" music. But it doesn't mean that Conrad, Tolstoy and Seth have failed. Only that you have.

So it's acceptable to reject the *Dance* because you don't like to read about Etonians, Oxford, debutante's balls, country house visits and the Ritz. It's not acceptable to say that the writer is therefore at fault. You're entitled to say that you'd prefer it if Powell had written about life in the Glasgow tenements or the slums of Mumbai or for that matter, the favelas of São Paolo. But you can't say that the choice of subject matter – something you find unsympathetic -- makes the novel itself bad.

I was on Radio 4's *A Good Read*, a panel-show in which each person has to choose a book, which is read and then discussed by everybody else. I chose *Casanova's Chinese Restaurant*. One fellow-guest quite liked it but "couldn't help wondering how many of the characters had private incomes". Sure, you are entitled not to like novels about people with private incomes, though that limits your choice somewhat. No Proust, for starters, and no PG Wodehouse either.

But this volume begins in a pub with Mr Deacon, Moreland, Maclintick, Gossage and Carolo: all of them hard up and all working for their living: a shopkeeper, two journalists and two musicians, plus Nick, dogbody in a publishing house. Perhaps Powell's reputation had given these saloon bar drinkers an aura of hidden wealth.

I hope, then, we can accept the fact that Powell is as entitled to write about Eton as I am entitled to write about Emanuel School near Clapham Junction (in its non-fee-paying days) and Dickens is entitled to write about people with no education at all. The problem – in terms of snobbery – comes if Powell puts Etonians above everybody else: if the tone of the novel is either cringing or resentful towards social superiors while despising or patronising perceived inferiors.

There is a theory that *Dance* depends for its movement and motivation on the snobbing of Widmerpool at school: rejected, bullied and despised for his social insignificance, he takes his revenge on the world in the course of the eleven volumes that follow. It's a good theory so long as you don't mistake of reading the actual books.

In fact Widmerpool is spoken of admiringly by Parkinson, the head of Games at the Le Bas house, and is treated with courtesy by Budd, the captain of the Eleven no less. His is mildly teased by Stringham and Templer, but nothing to which the most fastidious could object.

The theory continues that the derision excited by Widmerpool's overcoat is based on snobbish contempt for a poor boy doing his best in straightened circumstances. But he is never ragged about the overcoat: it's a laboured running joke that Widmerpool himself knows very little about. Another boy, Offord, has a similar overcoat, but nobody makes a fuss about it. It's not the overcoat that's the problem, it's Widmerpool.

And it's not the modesty of his background that's the problem. It's crucial to the entire sequence that Nick has an equally modest background. Neither has grand connections with the aristocracy, neither has much money by Etonian standards. They are neither of them stars: both are drab members of a glamorous school. Both must make their own way in the world as best they can. Each does so with different methods and priorities and it's that -- and not snobbery – that's the point, in some ways the point of the entire work.

Widmerpool's problem is not that he doesn't fit in at Eton. It's that he wouldn't fit in at Tulse Hill Comprehensive either, or for that matter, Emanuel. No matter what school he went to, he would be found wearing the wrong sort of overcoat – or making some other blunder that, trivial in others, is always remembered about him. It's not about overcoats, it's about Widmerpool.

It is, in short, about character. It's always about character -- but that's true of all novels, including *Finnegans Wake*. So let's look at some of the less privileged characters in *Dance*. I'll take one from each volume, which means the list will be far from encyclopaedic. Qualifications: the characters must be (a) non-Etonian, (b) non-Oxford (sorry Quiggin), (c) never invited to debutantes' dances, (d) not related by blood to aristocracy (e) not rich, or even well-off and (f) in general terms, altogether – to use a dated term – non-U.

1. Bum

Bum is, with Charlie, one of the two dogs who live at La Grenadière, where Nick goes to learn French. Now it's perfectly possible to be snobbish about non-human animals, as every horseperson knows, but Powell isn't snobbish about Bum – and in his dealings with the dog he reveals his approach to every character who steps into the pages of the book. And it's the same: human or non-human, aristocrat or commoner, Etonian or educated elsewhere.

He doesn't look down on Bum for being a dog, and a dog of no clear pedigree at that. Instead he discusses his situation in the way that we readers are, after two and a bit chapters, getting used to. With calm interest Nick/Powell looks down at the relationship between the two dogs, who live "in a state of perpetual war", and how Charlie picks a quarrel with Bum every seven days, on the day Bum has his bath, and his "crisp coat" is washed so that that looks "as if it were woven from a glistening thread of white pipe-cleaners".

These mild observations are not there for decoration. They play a part in the plot, for Powell is a master of the hideously difficult, complex and almost invariably overlooked art or craft of plotting a novel. Nick is helping Suzette to give Bum his bath when Bum escapes, and the resulting pursuit leads to a lightning-brief moment of hand-holding intimacy, a promising start interrupted by the arrival of Widmerpool.

In this tiny vignette, with this non-human character who plays the minutest part in the narrative, we get a gin-clear glimpse of Powell's easy and confident skill as a craftsman of the novel, along with his ungrudging half-ironical semidetached sympathy for -- and interest in -- all his characters, be they mongrel or earl.

2. Gypsy

Gypsy gets snobbed all right – but not by Nick or Powell. Moreland calls her "La Pasionaria of Hendon Central". Barnby says: "Jones is an excellent specimen of middleclass education brought to its logical conclusions", added that she is "literally... incapable of thought.

But Nick is not so hostile. We can put at least some of this down to the democratising power of lust. After a debutante ball with vacuous beauties like Margaret Budd, Jones's combative nature, short skirt and Eton crop are at least a refreshing change, showing different possibilities in womankind.

Gypsy in turn has a mild thing for Nick, in part driven by her "imperfectly concealed respect for 'books'." They flirt -- combatively -- at Mr Deacon's party: "Why are you so stuck up?" "I'm just made that way." All this paves the way to their encounter after Mr Deacon's funeral, one that apparently relieves Nick of the burden of his virginity – after which Nick's interest in her is magically extinguished: "Any wish to remain any longer present in these surroundings had suddenly and violently decreased, if not disappeared entirely".

Gypsy bewitches Widmerpool, who pays for her abortion and is in turn introduced by her to left-wing politics, so her part in the novel is crucial. After that she remains in the background, apparently well thought of by the Party, a friend, perhaps more than friend of Erridge, on her soap-box at the outbreak of war, later married to Craggs (Lady Craggs, no less) and liquidating the manuscript of Odo Stevens.

Gypsy is a character that any card-carrying snob would at once despise and fear: an uncomfortable aggressive presence from the less privileged classes (father a school teacher) who is a threat to any sort of privileged life. He would; seek out, exaggerate or invent a raft of despicable qualities. But Powell doesn't despise her. He writes her as a proper character, like Bum, Stringham and Erridge, Earl of Warminster. Powell is interested in her, and succeeds in making her interesting to us. She is not a caricature. You can walk all round her. And you can't write a proper character in a naturalistic novel from a basis of fear and loathing. There has to be more. A snob couldn't make her real. And Gypsy is real.

3. Mrs Erdleigh

Myra Erdleigh is the widow of a colonial official, perhaps Chinese customs or Burma police, and guest at the Ufford -- so she has neither money nor social position. She is a clairvoyant and fortune-teller. Dr Trelawney is described as being both absurd and threatening; Mrs Erdleigh is both absurd and dignified.

She's not a figure of fun, like Madam Sosostris in *The Waste Land*. Her predictions, when she first lays the cards out for Nick, are respectably accurate twice over. And though Nick is never exactly under her spell, he enjoys her very much.

What's more, he likes her. He always enjoys her company. He admires the way she soothes the intractable Mona, the way she takes charge with planchette. Much later in the sequence she shows courage when taking on Pam: "Court at your peril those spirits that dabble lasciviously with primeval matter, horrid substances, sperm of the world..."

It's as if she really understands Pam and knows why she can't live without destruction and death. Pam believes that only Mrs Erdleigh has realised that Ferrand-Seneschal died in flagrante with Pam. This confrontation between Pam and Mrs Erdleigh seems more than a collision of personalities. It can even, perhaps, be understood as a battle between good and evil on the pavements of Regent's Park. And we have no doubt who is good.

Mrs Erdleigh's dignity – for all her absurdities and affectations -- is essential to the plot. She must oppose Pam, and then remove Jimmy Stripling from the trouble "by more or less occult means". She needs some measure of supernatural credentials.

If Mrs Erdleigh is to work as she does in this naturalistic novel, both Nick and Powell must like her, without being over credulous. The reader must also like her and take pleasure in her for more than her comic potential. She has real value and important meaning. And a snobbish writer could never have achieved that.

4. Ted Jeavons

Jeavons not only comes from a dowdy background, he is also widely considered a bore. Widmerpool, Chips Lovell, Mrs Conyers, Mark members and Dicky Umfraville all agree. Lovell explains, with debonair snobbishness, how Molly met him when working as a car-polisher at the Motor show: "I can't remember what make, but not a car anyone would be proud to own."

But Nick likes him and finds him fascinating. Perhaps it's all about the way Jeavons married into the aristocracy without for a second changing his way of presenting himself to the world, still less having ambitions as a social climber.

As a result the two share the adventure of Umfraville's night club, in which Jeavons is reunited with Mildred Blaides, with whom he shared a brief dalliance in the First World War. He explains this to Nick: "I suppose it's a story a real gent wouldn't tell. But then I'm not a real gent." He comes out well in the implicit comparison with Widmerpool, who is Mildred's fiancé until things go so terribly wrong in the bedrooms of Dogdene.

Perhaps the line that matters most about Jeavons is his matter-of-fact acceptance of total war: "He felt at home within its icy grasp". He copes unexpectedly well with Molly's death and lets rooms in their place in South Kensington. Norman Chandler, one of his tenants, thinks the world of him.

So here is a character with meaning and mystery, enigmatic qualities, likeable, an adventurer in his way. He is a person of depth and subtlety: and it's impossible to draw a character like that if you think he is beneath you. The essential aspect of the way Powell draws characters in the *Dance* is by way of detached democratising sympathy. He gets the point of people. All kinds of people. Which is precisely what no snob can do.

5. Maclintick

This volumes takes us from discontent with life through to misery and onwards into despair. The character Powell chooses to show these terrible things to us is not a well-born poète maudit, nor a wealthy aristocrat who has drained life's heady cup to the lees. It's a pub-haunting journalist from Pimlico.

Maclintick is intelligent. At Casanova's Chinese Restaurant he contributes wittily to the debate on time and space and quotes appositely from *Henry IV Part One*. But his domestic life is a disaster: Nick's visit to the Maclintcks with Moreland is a revelation of horror. Husband and wife see the guests as an ideal audience for the drama of their mutual hatred.

Each is deeply disappointed by life and knows precisely where the blame lies. They are hard at it again at the party for Moreland's symphony: Nick suggests that they should leave off for once in a way, to give themselves greater energy for next time: but no doubt the audience is part of the point. Back home there is nothing but "bleak despair".

Mrs Maclintick then goes off with Carolo and precipitates Maclintick's final desolation. Nick is persuaded to join Moreland in another visit to that awful Pimlico house and it's at this point that Maclintick makes "the harrowing remark that established throughout all eternity his relationship with Moreland. 'I obey you, Moreland,' he said, 'with the proper respect of the poor interpretive hack for the true creative artist'."

The next time we hear of Maclintick he has gassed himself. Here is the mean death of a mean-spirited man in a mean house, one that is now full of gas, the lavatory blocked by the manuscript of Maclintick's unreadable masterwork on musicology – and here is all the tragedy of love mistook and a person utterly at odds with the world. Nick doesn't really like Maclintick: but he understands the pain and despair of his life. He is not too grand too spare a thought – many thoughts -- for a grouchy, impoverished loser.

6. Albert

Literature is full of servants, many of them comic. Sometimes they are smarter than their masters, like Figaro, Sancho Panza, Lear's Fool and Jeeves; sometimes they are bumbling but faithful, like Partridge (*Tom Jones*) and Samwise Gamgee (*The Lord of the Rings*). They tend to exist only in the context of their masters.

Albert is not like that. Being a servant is what he does, not what he is. He has a timorous nature, sees himself as perpetually persecuted by women, suffers from his "'feet'" – surely the best use of quotation mark in the entirety of the Dance – and has "a touch of narcissism to be found in some artists whatever their medium – for Albert was certainly an artist in cooking."

He appears first in the long flashback to Nick's childhood in the opening chapter of TKO, and in the third chapter he turns up again, now running a seaside hotel, "the same timorous, self-centred, sceptical artist-cook". Nick sees him affectionately and admiringly but quite without sentimentality.

Albert presides over the death of Uncle Giles, and subsequently the gloriously bizarre sequence in which Dr Trelawney the thaumaturge is locked in the bathroom and, once rescued, preaches to Nick and Duport until Mrs Erdleigh arrives with whatever calming substances he needs.

Albert plays a small part in the novel. In plot terms it is necessary for the maid Billson to love him, so triggering her breakdown, and for him to run the Bellevue. He could be restricted to a few standard traits of personality and comic quirks of diction while the action of the main characters of higher social classes goes about their business.

But Powell goes deeper, for that's the kind of novelist he is. Albert, for all his fleeting appearance, is a real character with dignity and meaning. He doesn't just make the mechanism of the plot function while supplying a cheap laugh: he enriches the volume he appears in, and so contributes to the power and vividness of the entire sequence.

7. Captain Gwatkin

Many heroes with dreams of military glory find themselves compromised by their feelings for a woman. Homer gives us Achilles, Shakespeare Mark Antony, Tolstoy Vronsky: all men of status. Powell gives us Captain Gwatkin, who worked in a bank and wasn't much good at it.

Gwatkin is not made ridiculous by this company, any more than Leopold Bloom is made ridiculous by the analogy with Odysseus in *Ulysses*. Rather we grasp the point that heroic aspirations are thoroughly democratic.

The seventh volume is about Gwatkin's ambitions of becoming a military paragon and his inability to realise them. He is bewildered to learn that dreams are not enough on their own: that mere keenness doesn't make him a brilliant officer, or even a competent one.

Nick's period of intimacy with Gwatkin is powerful and rich with meaning. In a groundsheet-cape and steel helmet, Gwatkin is transformed into "a figure from the later Middle Ages, a captain-of-arms of the Hundred Years War, or the guerrilla campaigning of Owen Glendower."

Gwatkin talks to Nick about his love for Kipling's poem *A Song to Mithras*, with its vision of soldiering as a lofty destiny. But on training exercises and the affair of Bithel's drunkenness he reveals his inefficiency and his inability to grasp military realities – and then he falls in love with Maureen the barmaid.

His predicament is both banal and profound, with elements of both tragedy and comedy. Gwatkin is ridiculous; he is also dignified. Finally, at the end, unstuck, losing his battalion and finding Maureen in the arms of Corporal Gwylt, he at least has the courage and detachment to laugh. "I felt I had not been wrong in thinking there was some style about him."

Gwatkin is not inadequate as an officer because he is from the wrong social class. Kedward, from much the same sort of background, takes over and apparently does a very decent job. Gwatkin's fall is about the disconnect between dreams and realities: and if that doesn't make him a universal character I don't know what else could.

8. Bithel

There are aristocrats and Etonians and dancers at debutante balls, even a few well-bred officers and certainly endless members of the Tolland family: and yet one of the most memorable characters in the entire sequence is this small-town misfit who looked as if he had just "done something perfectly disgusting, and was pretty sure he was about to be detected...."

Bithel doesn't fit any form of stock character, with his gentleness, respect for learning, almost apologetic deceitfulness, bibulousness and with a vast talent for getting into scrapes. He makes his first appearance in the previous volume, surrounded by rumours that he once played rugby for Wales; his subsequent performance with the dummy in his bed is the best dance in the pages of *Dance*.

In the eighth volume he talks disconnectedly during an air-raid about identifying with the heroes in *Boys' Own Paper* and a cheque of his that bounced. Private Stringham come under his command at the Mobile Laundry and is treated very decently, enough to win Stringham's gratitude and an attempt to rescue him when he

247

has fallen drunk in the street. But Widmerpool has him out of the army: and boasts about it distastefully.

Bithel is appealing, both guilty and innocent at the same time, hopelessly incapable at dealing with life but managing to muddle along, always one step from the next disaster. He turns up again in the final volume, rescued from dereliction by Scorp Murtlock. This reunites him with Widmerpool, who must undertake a series of terrible penances for the wrongs he did Bithel 30 years earlier. Bithel has almost the last word in the entire sequence as he announces the death of Widmerpool.

Only a genius could have written Bithel. If Bithel is despicable, he is never despised: instead he exemplifies the absurdity of military life, and of life in any context. Could a snob have written him?

9. Odo Stevens

When you're writing a 12-volume novel, your minor characters can be developed as fully as the major characters in novels of conventional length. Not only can be: must be. If you can't, again and again, make your characters full, round and interesting, the ultra-marathon distance is not for you.

Odo Stevens demonstrates this principle as well as any of the second-tier characters in *Dance*.

He's an oafish hero, a little too confident in his ability to make a conquest of one and all, especially if female. He's from Birmingham and speaks fluent Brum. Any decent novelist could write him up just like that, and he would play his part in the plot just fine. That's how he appears in VB, the first war volume.

But Powell is in it for the long-haul and has no option but to go deeper. When Stevens turns up at the Café Royal in the next volume he reveals himself as a music-lover and Moreland fan, and the writer of a melancholy poem. He is "narcissistic... but not narrowly egotistical. He was interested in everything round him, even though everything must eventually lead back to himself."

He emerges from the war as a hero, showing that wars are not necessarily won by sensitive responses and gentlemanly manners. By BDFR he's an author of a spicy war memoir, outwitting even Gypsy Jones in direct action to get it published. By TK he is rather subdued, married to Rosie Manasch and with a passion for vintage cars, hooting with apparent derision as Widmerpool walks off into exile.

Dance is a naturalistic novel, narrated by a detached observer. Therefore it lives or dies by the depth of its characters. If Powell had been a snob he would have written Odo as a two-dimensional lout full of comic Brummie locutions

– and few of us would read all 12 volumes, still less gone back to the beginning to start again.

10. X Trapnel

Dance is full of tragic heroes and heroines trying to come to terms with the fact that they're caught up in a comedy. Examples: Stringham, Templer, Maclintick, Erridge, Gwatkin, Moreland, Pricilla, Pam. And of course X Trapnel.

It's essential for both the plot and the tone of this volume that Trapnel is (a) a highly gifted writer and (b) socially undistinguished. He needs to be out of his league socially with Pam, at the same time accepted by people in the literary world as a writer on the brink of a masterpiece. The literary world depicted here is seedy, down at heel and meeting in pubs, but doing all it can to revive British culture now the war is at last over.

Pubs are Trapnel's natural milieu, and even in his cups, he fills the saloon bar with good sense about literature. His life is full of fantasy and role-playing, but it's clear that his work is uncompromisingly rooted in reality. Trapnel is worth the (considerable) trouble if you believe good writing matters: that's why Nick takes him on.

But Trapnel is a high-wire act. Without wealth or social position or talent for anything except writing, he is vulnerable. Despite his apparent triumph over the Widmerpools in the penultimate chapter, it is simplicity itself for them to bring about his destruction in the last.

Trapnel, son of an itinerant jockey, roams from pub to pub and one uncomfortable low-rent or no-rent dwelling to another. He is a novelist's triumph: his fall would have no meaning if the author failed to make vivid all that is best in him.

11. Audrey Maclintick

Nick the observer doesn't like her. But Powell the novelist makes us aware of her better qualities, as well as of the complexities and contradictions in her make-up. If there are hints of snobbishness in Nick's attitude, there are none in Powell's presentation of her.

We first meet her in CCR at the Pimlico flat she shares with her husband, and witness the horrible row, for which both are equally to blame. They're in the thick of another at Mrs Foxe's party – but then Audrey is swept off her feet by Stringham, and this fearsome lady becomes nothing less than kittenish. And so far as Stringham at least is concerned, sexy.

She runs off with Carolo, her husband kills himself, and Moreland and Gossage are left to do the clearing up. But in SA she is living with Moreland. She is still truculent at their meeting at the Café Royal, but we begin to see her good points. Nick muses that in terms of Moreland's self-confessed "retreat from perfectionism"; his alliance with Audrey (after Matilda and Priscilla) was "an operation reasonably to be designated a rout". The reader is inclined to think: steady on a bit. Audrey is doing a good job. Without her, Moreland would be in poor shape, and we like Moreland.

She turns up again in TK, more sympathetic again, still Moreland's minder, and prepared to take on anyone who gets in the way of her doing so. Nick's antipathy to her is important: those terrible rows work because Nick is appalled by both Maclinticks, especially Audrey. But the novelist sees further than his own narrator: as a result, we who do the reading see Audrey more clearly than Nick can. The message to snob-hunters is this: don't confuse Nick Jenkins with Anthony Powell. They're not always the same.

12. Scorp Murtlock

This last volume is concerned, among other matters, with the end of Widmerpool and it's haunted by *The Revenger's Tragedy*. So who does Powell recruit as Widmerpool's nemesis, the man who takes revenge on Widmerpool on behalf of – among many others – Nick, Stringham, Templer, Duport, Farebrother, Trapnel, Bagshaw, Pam, Glober, Gwinnett, Bithel, Hogbourne-Johnson, Moreland and Tokenhouse?

The answer is the son of a newsagent. Scorp Murtlock is not some high-born representative of imaginative or poetic truth, nor is he a ludicrous form of low-life, whose apparent inappropriateness turns out to be appropriate.

Murtlock is dignified, plausible, frightening as well as faintly absurd. He expresses himself well in his own idiom. He is an imposing figure: he has to be or Widmerpool wouldn't have fallen for him and been bested by him.

Murtlock's power, as he walks across the field at Stourwater in the manner of Apollyon, is clearly a thing to behold. It takes an awful lot to oppose him: Barnabas only manages it because Chuck is with him. Earlier Fiona left the cult, but only at the cost of taking part in the rite of the Devil's Fingers, and she had Delvacquerie's support. Widmerpool tries to leave, but his wish is refused. Murtlock won't have it. Widmerpool, a man who has always lived by the will, is beaten by a young hippy whose will is stronger than his own. He leaves the gathering at Stourwater as a man whose end can't be far away.

The book ends with Bithel's account of Widmerpool's death: and that one is one where apparent inappropriateness becomes wholly appropriate. But Bithel too must return to Murtlock.

If there are one or two false notes in the drawing of Murtlock, they are of incomprehension over generations rather than social classes. Small example: Murtlock's hair was "uncared for"; in point of fact hippies (I was there) mostly went in

253

for elaborate or at least regular hair-washing. You looked such a fool otherwise. Murtlock's hair would have rippled.

Murtlock is not a sympathetic character, but he's not supposed to be. He needs to be imposing, and when he needs to be, quite overwhelming. Credibly overwhelming. If he is to work as a character the novelist must write in a certain amount of respect, even a hint of fear, from his narrator. Snobbish contempt would have destroyed this volume and with it the last few miles of the ultra-marathon. The fact is that Powell is more interested in writing a good novel than in scoring social points: and that has been the case from first lines of QU to the last of HSH.

*

I have, I hope, made a decent case for demonstrating that *A Dance to the Music of Time* is not a work of snobbery. If Powell was a snob in his private life, as some have claimed, (I never met him but had a couple of very friendly comms) he was not a snob as a novelist. He needed all his non-U characters to live and breathe and speak and act, not as caricatures but as characters who live – for often they have a pretty long life, turning up in volume after volume. Sure, a snob could have written *Dance* – and it would have been bloody awful.

That leaves us with a final question. If *Dance* is not a snobbish work, who do so many people insist that it is? Why are the same people prepared to praise the unquestionably snobbish *Brideshead* while rejecting Powell?

The answer is staring us in the face. *Dance* is a bloody long work, one that requires serious commitment. How much simpler if you could be let off reading it -- and come up with a reason for doing so that shows off your own integrity, good taste and nobility of soul?

So you read the first chapter of the first volume, about Eton and the half the next, set at Mrs Foxe's grand house – and then give up, without ever meeting Bum, Gyspy, Myra, Ted, Maclintick, Albert, Rowland, Bith, Odo, X, Audrey and Scorp, somehow convinced that your own life is richer for missing out.

The fact of the matter is that those who complain that *Dance* is snobbish are only confessing their own lack of literary endurance. And that's no sin. Fine. Go away and read something more trivial if you wish. Just don't blame the author.

Acknowledgements

Thanks to the Anthony Powell Society for existing and for keeping the conversation going for a quarter of a century. Thanks to Keith Marshall for founding it and for keeping me up to the mark when it's been necessary. Thanks to Stephen Walker, editor of the *Newsletter*, for accepting and publishing my contributions. Thanks to Robin Bynoe for suggesting that we put the pieces together and taking on all the niggling and thankless tasks that this involves. Thanks to all members of the Anthony Powell Society for keeping the faith.

The Author

Simon Barnes spoke at the first APS conference at Eton in 2001. His subject was Anthony Powell and drink, under the title *A Dance to the Music of Time, Gentlemen, Please*. He has written more than 30 non-fiction books, mostly on sport and wildlife. He has also written four novels. He worked for *The Times* for 32 years, latterly as chief sportswriter while also writing two weekly wildlife columns. He lives in Norfolk with his family, where he manages an area of marshland for wildlife.